Seriously Mum, What's an Alpaca?

Alan Parks

Book 1 of the *Seriously Mum* series

Table of Contents

Some character names in this book have been
changed to preserve anonymity.

Introduction

To say that my life has changed over the last few years would be a drastic understatement. I have been through the wettest winters and the hottest summers imaginable.

I share my beautiful home in the Andalucían hills with a menagerie of strange creatures. The inquisitive alpacas are a joy to be around, but, to be honest, the dogs can be a nightmare. I do my best to keep out of their way. Sometimes, just to be annoying, I like to walk past their fence. Sometimes I just sit there and stare at them, which really irritates them, especially the big one!

When the chickens arrived I thought maybe they would be good for dinner one day. But I just can't do it. I can't imagine eating them.

I enjoy my siestas by the pool, during the long, hot summer. If I can keep away from the kids for an hour or two, then the peace and quiet is fantastic.

When we have visitors it's always exciting. It means dinner will be something interesting. Hopefully the guests will have brought something special for me.

Since those two strange people came to live here with us, I have had eight babies, and the last four left home not so long ago. This year's were a handful, but I coped, I always do. As it's winter, I spend most of the time in the barn, trying to keep warm in the hay.

But soon it will be spring, the sun will shine and the birds will be back. Then it will be my favourite time of year, when the baby birds are hatching. Then dinner will be easy to get. Then I can return to my lazy life by the pool.

Barb (Feral Cat)

Chapter 1
Crazy Idea

Animal Count: One dog (Geri)

"Okay, tell me a bit more about this idea then," said Lorna, as we battled against the wind on the seafront near Brighton. It was a couple of days since her revelation.

"Well, I've been thinking. Why don't we move somewhere else? You know, try something different? It would take the pressure off you, get you out of dancing, and also be something exciting and new for us."

Two days earlier, on a previous walk, Lorna had told me that she was struggling to keep up with teaching at her dance school.

"I'm not sure how long I can go on," she had said.

She had been diagnosed with Sarcoidosis and Thyroiditis, after nearly two years of doctor's visits and hospital appointments. It was making work difficult and taking its toll on all of us.

"Hmm, okay," she said, "but what would we do? I don't know how to be anything other than a dance teacher. And you've only ever worked in shops. We can't just drop everything and do something else."

"Do you remember that funny looking animal we saw at Prague zoo? The alpaca?"

Lorna gave me a puzzled look, as though I'd lost my marbles. "Yes, of course. We loved him, but what's that got to do with anything?"

"Well, I've been doing a bit of research, and it looks like alpacas are quite a profitable business. I was thinking maybe we could breed them. Maybe move to Florida and do it?"

Lorna was giving me a look that said, "I can't believe we are even talking about this!" I knew I was pushing my

6

luck with the Florida suggestion, but I was serious about the alpacas.

"No way! I can't move to Florida, Alan. What about the kids? It's too far! Visiting would be expensive and you know how I hate flying! It's nine hours to Florida!" Lorna's two children, Mark, (24 at the time), happily living with his girlfriend, and Frankie, 18, and very close to her Mum, evidently put Florida out of the question.

"Okay, okay," I sighed. "I thought you might say that. What about Spain?"

"Spain? Really? But you've never even been there! And you don't like the heat. How would you cope?"

"I'd be okay, I would get used to it. I think we should move away and do something completely different."

"Hmm..."

"Frankie and her boyfriend could even come with us," I suggested.

"Well, I need to do something. I can't carry on like I am at the moment. In tears one minute and having to put on a smile the next. Plus, if I give up teaching, I don't want always to be known as 'Lorna the dance teacher' when we see people around town."

"Have a think about it then," I said. "The house should be easy to sell."

Our house was situated in a desirable area, just outside Brighton, on top of cliffs, with a 180 degree sea view.

Near our house was a country park, open to the public, which houses a sizeable number of llamas and alpacas. We decided to head there, to have a look around, and to think more about our idea. It is a beautiful place and we sat outside the cafe, in the sunshine, staring at the alpacas. It was that day that we fell in love with them.

We wandered into the barn, where the babies were being kept for the first delicate days of their lives, before being released into the fields. One particular alpaca, Poppy, who had been orphaned the year before, wandered freely about. She had been hand-reared and was very friendly, nuzzling up under our arms for a cuddle. Curiosity attracted other alpacas too, who came to have a look, and take a little food from our hands before running away again. They were relaxing to watch and totally bewitching.

"Could we really do this?" Lorna asked.

"I think we could. Obviously we will have to do some research to find out more about them. But just imagine, what could be better than a life in the sun with these beautiful animals as companions?"

"You know what they say, never work with children or animals. Well, I've spent 30 years teaching children, why not complete the set?"

"Well, what do you think? Is it a yes?"

"Oh my God! I think it is!" Lorna laughed nervously.

So that was it. We would move to Spain and breed alpacas.

Chapter 2
What's an Alpaca?

"Hi, Frankie, we need to talk to you," Lorna said as her daughter came in through the front door. She'd been staying at her boyfriend's house, and Lorna had called to say she wanted her to come home.

"What's wrong? What have I done?" was Frankie's first reaction.

"Nothing's wrong, Frankie. We just need to talk to you about something. Something quite big."

Lorna explained about her illness and how difficult work had been during the past year. Frankie knew bits and pieces because she had been helping her Mum teach the classes, but I don't think she realised the full extent of the problem.

"We've been talking, and we think now is a good time for me to give up the dance school. We're thinking of moving away, possibly to Spain, to do something different. Now, you have three options. First, you and Chris could come along and help us. Or you could stay here and take over the dance school. If you wanted to, of course. Or you might want to do something else?"

Frankie looked horrified and burst into tears. After a few minutes, she gathered herself together again. "Okay then, when do we go?" was followed quickly by, "You said, 'do something different'. What would we do?"

"Well, we're thinking about breeding alpacas," Lorna said.

"Bloody hell, Mum! What's an alpaca?" asked Frankie through her tears. So Lorna explained.

Breaking the news to Mark was no less emotional, but it was a little easier. He was living with his girlfriend and was settled. He wished us luck; his first reaction was "Great, free holidays!"

9

Over the next few weeks we spent hours on the Internet researching these beautiful animals. We were fascinated by stories of people around the world, giving up successful careers to breed them, enjoying a fantastic lifestyle, and making pots of money too.

We spent a day on an 'Alpaca Experience' in Devon, and the more we learned, the more we felt it was a possibility. Alpacas are enchanting. Every farmer, breeder and enthusiast we spoke to was full of positivity, both for alpacas as an industry, and for our idea too. Neither Lorna nor I had any experience with livestock, but Lorna's family had always kept dogs and I grew up in a house with a couple of cats. However, we were assured, "It doesn't matter if you have never been a farmer, these animals are easy to look after. They don't get sick and they are cheap to feed." Our research and farm visits backed this up. This lifestyle seemed so idyllic and perfect that we just wanted so much to be a part of it.

The next stage was to find a suitable location to carry out the plan that was beginning to formulate in our heads. These days, with the Internet, there are so many properties out there to choose from. Something for everyone; from a rural idyll in the Slovakian hills, to a modern penthouse in Budapest, all at the touch of a button. Our choice of Spain was twofold; accessibility and abundant sunshine. There are cheap flights from most UK airports, important for family visits and emergencies, should they arise, and of course, Spain is renowned for its sunshine.

During our Internet research, we stumbled across Peter and Penny in Andalucía. They had transported their herd of alpacas from the UK to Spain to launch the industry there. We made contact and arranged to meet them during a viewing trip.

Chapter 3
An Assortment of Viewings

Initially I made the decision, rightly or wrongly, to do the exploring trip on my own, because I felt that Lorna would say 'yes' to almost anything, just to get out of the current situation. We didn't have a specific location in mind, but we had two main criteria: land and character. The land was a necessity, but we dreamed of something remote and full of character.

Having visited and discounted an eco-project near Barcelona, in July I made a trip to Andalucía, where it was planned that I would visit a few properties in different areas. They ranged from Malaga to Cordoba, Ronda to Cadiz.

I was met from the airport by the first estate agent, Malcolm. An archetypal English gentleman, dressed in khaki shorts that were slightly too short and a blue checked shirt, he had the glow of a man who spent too much time in the sun, emphasised by the whiteness of his hair. On his feet he wore sandals, accompanied by brown ankle-length socks. Malcolm was in his 60s and was accompanied by his 'Marbella-style' wife, Angela, at least 20 years his junior, all blonde hair and make up and carrying the essential Chihuahua. I was quite taken aback by the stereotypical 'expatness' of the couple.

"Nice to meet you Alan." He marched towards me with outstretched hand. "This is Angela, and Pepper."

As we walked towards the car, Malcolm said to me, "I've got a few beautiful places to show you. You are going to love them. We are going to head towards Coin, and Alhaurin el Grande."

Unbeknown to me at the time, these towns are little expat communities where one can walk no more than a few metres down the road without bumping into an

English person.

We drove out of the hustle and bustle of Malaga, and started to climb the hills behind the city. We soon reached the town of Coin.

"Here we go, Alan, this is where you want to be, Fish and Chips over here, Chinese restaurant round the corner, and there, just there, is the Irish bar where everybody goes at the weekend."

The thought made me shudder. It was so not what we wanted. When we had been discussing the move, we had decided that if we were going to move to Spain, it would be somewhere that was the 'real' Spain, where we would need to try and learn Spanish, and integrate ourselves into the community as much as possible.

"Erm, Malcolm, I'm not really sure this is what we are looking for."

"Of course it is Alan, wait and see. This place will blow you away."

We pulled up outside a white box of a house, with a fenced-in garden, and all of about 200 square metres of garden, including a swimming pool. The house was nice inside, as you would expect, but my brief had been for land for the animals.

"Where will we put the alpacas?" I asked.

"In the garden, there's loads of room!"

I had emailed the agents exactly what we were looking for, in terms of land and housing, but obviously they decide what and where they want to take you. During the boom years, hundreds of these white boxes, with very little character, were thrown up to cope with the influx of expats into the towns.

Malcolm said to me "You have to be flexible, if you want to live in this area, you may need to do some work. My house hasn't even had a roof for four months. Been sleeping under the stars, we have."

"To be honest then Malcolm, this isn't the area for us. If you can't show us something with a few acres of land, and a bit of character, then we won't be doing business I'm afraid."

I couldn't believe this estate agent had just told me that even his own house didn't have a roof; it didn't exactly fill me with confidence. On the plus side, on the journey back to the airport, Malcolm only fell asleep once at the wheel, veering sharply toward the barrier as Angela poked him sharply in the ribs to wake him. My first day in Andalucía, hadn't gone very well.

The following day I caught the bus to Ronda, located in the mountains behind Malaga. This journey involved a treacherous two-hour journey on winding mountain roads, with a speedy bus driver. Hair-raising overtaking manoeuvres had me gripping on to my seat with white knuckles, whilst the predominantly Spanish passengers surrounding me seemed oblivious to the danger.

When I arrived, I was met by John, the local agent. We took a quick detour into the town of Ronda to see the solicitor he dealt with. The solicitor happened to be an English-speaking man who was very smart and came across as friendly and helpful. His name was José and I took a card, in case we needed him later on for anything.

We then went and had breakfast in a bar. The first thing one notices is the Spanish men, who are all drinking brandy first thing in the morning. Then most of them get in their cars to go and work on the land.

We then headed to John's office in a small town just outside Ronda called Arriate. John was a bit more suave than Malcolm, being attired in a white linen outfit with brown leather sandals. We went to his office, and spent some time looking through the properties on his website, but, although the properties were more in keeping with the style we were looking for, rural and tranquil, the prices were far higher than Lorna and I had anticipated. After a leisurely lunchtime beer (or two) and tapas, we ventured out to see the only property that I felt was worthy of inspection. It was in need of renovation, but had plenty of space, and land in abundance for the alpacas.

The property we went to see was in the mountains of the 'Sierra de Ronda' and was described as a fully-fenced finca, currently being used as a goat farm, with living accommodation. As we drove up the increasingly winding road, the view across the mountains was awe-inspiring. A landscape full of mountainsides and valleys, punctuated by pine trees, while in the distance the sea was glistening in the sunlight. Just as I was admiring the view from the window, we veered off the road and onto 200 metres of dusty track. Even in John's 4x4 we were bouncing up and down and banging our heads on the roof of the car. We pulled up outside the house.

The gate (for want of a better word), was in actual fact two single metal bed frames, end to end, fastened in the middle with a chain. Slightly hesitantly, I followed John towards the house. The level of work needed here seemed to be huge. It was a good size, and had three buildings of different levels spread around a central terrace. All were in a state of disrepair; paint and render falling off walls. There was a roof missing from one building and where the electricity had been connected, there were bare wires running from building to building. There was what looked like a swimming pool that had been left to go a slime-green colour, like a badly kept duck pond.

The owner of the house emerged, and I was introduced to Pepe, then Pepe's wife emerged and then his mother. His daughter and her husband followed and then his son. There were also three small children hanging around. The Spanish contingent just kind of stared at John and I, while Pepe removed his hat and shook my hand with gusto. *"Buenas tardes, señores"* he said humbly.

For the rest of the visit both John and I were *"señores"*. As we were talking, Pepe was very animated in his enthusiasm for the house, and he was obviously very proud of his little country *finca*. Not wanting to insult the family, I gestured that I liked the house very much, and Pepe smiled the biggest, toothiest grin you can imagine.

The ice broken, John led the way, "Alan, remember it's all about potential," he said.

I followed John through the first door, and was shadowed by the six adults and three children. There was a tiny living room, centred around a fireplace on one wall, and on the other side of the room, a huge, old fashioned, shiny wooden sideboard with a portable TV right in the middle, in pride of place. There were two sets of plastic patio furniture arranged around the TV viewing area. The house didn't feel clean and it was very dark. I hadn't at that time cottoned on to the fact that the old country houses were built with small windows and thick walls to keep out the heat in the summer. Of course we, in the UK are used to having lots of light.

I smiled to John through gritted teeth, and said, "Hmmm, okay." There were three bedrooms, a very rustic-style kitchen, in the traditional Andalucían style with curtains instead of cupboard doors, and a very basic bathroom, all furnished in the same basic manner. We were even shown a room that had in the past been used for storing pig innards in the days where the family would gather and slaughter the pig they had been raising and then use it to make as many pork products as possible.

John explained that this was their weekend house, and where they would do their work. The animals would be kept here, and they would use the land to grow food and earn some income. The final room, under the bedrooms at the back of the house, was a large stable in which around 100 smelly goats lived. Yes, in the house! John explained that in the old days, before electricity, the heat from the animals was used to heat the upstairs rooms. Even though electricity had been connected since, they still lived in this traditional manner.

Outside there were chickens running around, peacocks showing off, various breeds of birds, all in different handmade aviaries attached to trees. There were a few loose sheep and dogs everywhere you looked. The pool turned out to be the water deposit, into which their well water flowed. Water came into the house at certain times and needed to be contained, but then had to be manually carried in to the house when required as they hadn't updated the plumbing system since the electricity had been installed. I was all for a bit of a fixer-upper but this was too much for me and I needed to get out for some air.

Lorna and I were not ready for a project of this size.

Once we said our protracted goodbyes to the whole family, the next port of call was going to be to the alpaca breeders.

John knew about the alpaca plan, in fact he was friends with the only alpaca breeders in Andalucia at the time, Peter and Penny, whom I had made contact with. He had even found them the land on which to build their house. John drove me to their farm, and I found a magnificent house in the final stages of being built, situated on a hilltop, overlooking a valley, with about four Alpaca paddocks at the bottom. It was stunning!

I was introduced to Peter first, who greeted us at the parking area next to the house. An older gentleman, he shook hands with me firmly and welcomed me with a warm smile.

"Come in and have a drink," he said. Peter reminded me of a headmaster, brimming with knowledge and experience, and of course very well-spoken.

I met Penny, his larger-than-life wife, and she threw her arms around me as if we had known each other for years. "How wonderful to meet you, luvvie!"

I spent a bit of time at the house with the two P's, Peter and Penny and the animals and spoke about our 'idea'. I explained that we had done some research, and liked the idea of breeding alpacas for a living, and also we had thought we might like to move to Spain. We didn't know if this would be possible, but we'd heard about them from the Internet, and were excited to find out more.

This farm seemed the ideal place to buy our alpacas from, and they were obviously very welcoming, to everyone! Whilst I was at their house, there was a constant trickle of people in and out, all English, and all helping themselves constantly to food and drink from the fridge. This feeling of 'community' made me think that the area might not be right for our project: we would be happy to have a few English families around us, but we did not want to be coerced into joining in with community activities, simply because of a common language. I don't think we would have mixed with many of these people at home, so we should not feel forced to by circumstances. We wanted to be able to keep ourselves to ourselves if we chose to.

I was, however, excited. "Next time Lorna and I visit for a house viewing trip, we will come and make another visit to see you," I promised, as I was leaving.

"You must stay over for a night when you come, we can have a barbecue!"

"That would be lovely," I replied. I left them with a feeling that this could really be a possibility.

The third and final day of my whirlwind visit to Andalucía dawned, and so far, none of the properties I had seen was close to fulfilling our needs.

Chapter 4
The Olive Mill

I was due to be meeting Sarah, an agent I had contacted by email, who dealt exclusively with rural property in Andalucía.

There was one particular property in her portfolio that had grabbed our attention, and I was due to see it today. It was a large, renovated Olive Mill, situated in the north of the province of Cordoba amongst the olive groves in the countryside, close to a town called Montoro. Sarah phoned me that morning to say she had hurt her back at another appointment and was unable to meet me. She had, however, arranged for her associate to accompany me, and to collect me from the train station.

Antonio was waiting for me when I got off the train in Cordoba. He was very jumpy and somewhat hyperactive with a Mediterranean complexion and dyed black hair that gave way to grey roots. There were large, dark rings around his eyes. I think the image was meant to be one of an international playboy, although it came across, in the harsh light of day, as more mid-life crisis!

"Alan, hi! Get in, this is my friend's van. My car is in the garage. Don't worry the brakes are bad, but it's fine. C'mon!"

"Okay, nice to meet you."

We tore out of the city and onto the motorway. For the entire 45-minute journey, Antonio never stopped talking, a well-rehearsed sales spiel of beautiful Spanish women, cheap food and drink and wonderful countryside (all of which are completely true, by the way). Eventually, we turned off the motorway onto a tarmac road. After 12 kilometres of country road, we turned on to a dusty track and seemed to start travelling even faster. Antonio was showing off, as obviously the track was used by only a few cars, but for three kilometres we were taking blind corners without looking, and the van slid through the dust. I was thankful to arrive at the Olive Mill in one piece!

As I exited the car, all I could see was a bit of a building site. The current owners, Neil and Caroline, were in the midst of renovating the courtyards, so there were pallets of bricks and piles of sand and cement everywhere you looked. There was also a menagerie of animals, horses, donkeys, dogs, cats, chickens, ducks, plus a huge pot-bellied pig.

Antonio stood back and stated, rather arrogantly, "The house sells itself, so why don't you get me a drink, Caroline," and he picked her up in his arms and carried her off, while she screamed like a little girl. So it was Neil who was left to show me around.

I liked Neil right away. He was a bit of a wide boy, wearing three-quarter length trousers, a white vest and a solid gold chain around his neck. He was a real down-to-earth joker, originally from Yorkshire, and had the sense of humour to go with it. He had a twitch in one of his eyes and he also squeaked. That is to say, that when he spoke, an involuntary squeaking sound came out of his mouth as well. I am not to this day sure how or why it happened, but as we were walking around, the squeaking became more and more obvious. To add to this, some top teeth were missing to leave only the middle one showing, he had a bit of a 'cowboy' limp, and the combination made it all seem slightly surreal.

"Come on then Alan, eek, let me show you around, eek eek."

I was given the tour. We went in through a small courtyard, created to make a feature of the huge, original olive-crushing stones. The conical stones were balanced on a large, circular, granite plinth, and would have been used in the days before machinery to produce the oil from the olives. This gave a fantastic first impression and was much more in keeping with the kind of place Lorna and I had been discussing.

We took the stairs up to an apartment, and went

through the old wooden door to a large room with a high vaulted ceiling, and a huge log-burning fireplace. There were even hooks left in the roof beams, from which the old farmers would have hung their homemade chorizo and sausages. The 'kitchenette' was small, but everything was there, and there were three huge bedrooms.

Everything needed decorating, but there was plenty of character. The owners had done a great job of putting in plenty of 'antiquey', rustic style furniture and ornaments to give it a well-dressed feeling and enhance the look.

Below the apartment was the storage room for the batteries, in which the power that was produced by the solar panels on the roof was stored. This fascinated me, and they seemed to have plenty of appliances, fridges, and even televisions in lots of rooms (We since found out that many of these had just been for dressing as well, as there are only a few TV aerial points in the house).

Next, we went through a large, rustic wooden gate, out to an enormous cobbled terrace where the olives would have been stored prior to pressing. This was where a motley selection of rescued stray dogs lived, and at the end of the terrace was a fabulous pair of wrought iron gates. There were numerous ancient wooden gates, which led off to the land in different areas, and also to an old stable that would have been used to house the mules and donkeys that powered the old mill stones.

Back through the large gate we went, into a room that had been used as a garage until Neil had arrived. He had fixed the roof and put some double doors on, and was in the process of fitting out the room to make a large central kitchen space, which could be the focal point of all the buildings. From the back of this room, there was a large ruined area, with two high walls that would have been used as housing for the olive workers originally. It was overgrown with weeds, and seemed to be a bit of a dumping place for old appliances and plastic oil containers. But... this had potential.

Beyond the ruined area there was a large, flat space which seemed perfectly situated for a pool. There was a huge eucalyptus tree that would provide ample shade in the hot months of summer. Adjacent to the 'pool area' was an old pig-sty which would make a lovely pool room, with shower and toilet. There was so much potential in this beautiful old place, it was difficult to take it all in. I met Mary-Belle, the Vietnamese pot-bellied pig, and I fell in love with her, she was beautiful. Sort of! Lorna and I are very much animal lovers, and part of the attraction of a rural life was to be able to have more animals around. I could just see us having a pig like Mary-Belle!

I completely fell in love with the Olive Mill: the ambience and the tranquility of the surroundings had me hooked, and because they already had horses there, I thought there would be adequate space for a small herd of alpacas. Although I loved it, I tried not to give too much away as I didn't want to seem over-keen. After about an hour at the Mill, Antonio took me back to the railway station in Cordoba, at breakneck speed, garbling on about some rich Russians he was making a deal with, or something similar.

I texted Lorna saying simply, 'It's amazing', and headed back to the hotel. I knew I needed Lorna to see it. I flew back home the following morning, knowing that if she loved the house as much as I did, it could be our new home; our new life!

On my return I said to Lorna, "Oh my God, the place is amazing! It's a bit of a drive from the airport, but I think it might be worth it. This could be the one!"

"Really? Oh wow!" she said. "Well, in that case, I'd better see it!"

Chapter 5
Lorna's Decision

We arranged for the second viewing to be as soon as Lorna finished work for the summer holidays, as we realised that if we were going to go ahead with our plan, we would need the summer holidays to finalise lots of things, like decorating and marketing the house in England. We organised a hire car, planning to drive abroad for the first time in our lives, and also booked to stay in the hotel in Montoro so we could see a bit of the town during our visit.

We flew out in the last week of July (probably the hottest time of the year, as we know now) and arranged to see the Olive Mill the following morning. Having never driven abroad before, I was nervous about both driving on the right side, and sitting on the left. After sitting in the car for a few minutes to get my bearings, we headed out on to the road and immediately there was traffic entering a roundabout from about six different exits. I was petrified. Once we were out of the airport vicinity, driving in Spain proved a breeze, a much more pleasant experience than in the UK.

I am sure any couple that has taken to foreign roads for the first time will have experienced my next three hours… "You're too close to the edge!" or "You nearly hit that car!" or even "You're driving in the middle of the motorway!"

Much to Lorna's relief we arrived in Montoro in one piece and what we found was exactly what we had expected, a little town, with whitewashed houses. There were old women cleaning their front steps, tractors driving up and down the roads, and even teenage boys chatting on a street corner sitting on the back of a horse.

When we arrived at the only hotel in town, we were pleasantly surprised to find it was relatively modern and the staff spoke a little English too. We quickly found our room and noticed the view from the balcony was absolutely stunning. Montoro is situated on the banks of the Rio Guadalquivir. The river wound across the scene underneath the balcony. On the left hand side, houses seemed to cling to the hillside, in a precarious higgledy-piggledy manner. There was an old Roman bridge and church towers in the distance. This felt like the location we had been looking for. A true Spanish town! We sat for hours that evening on the balcony, watching the swallows and bats dancing in the sky catching insects as the sun set over the town, creating beautiful reds, pinks and oranges in the sky. Perfect!

"Do you think we could really live here?" Lorna asked quietly.

"Why not?" I replied, and we sat, hand in hand, watching the sun disappear.

The following morning, we arranged to meet Antonio, and I explained to Lorna how he was a bit of a playboy wannabe, and not to take too much notice of him, and just concentrate on the Olive Mill. We met in a pre-arranged car park, and he insisted we climb into his newly acquired, racing green, boy's toy, open top Jeep Wrangler. Bear in mind, in July the daytime temperature is well over 40 degrees, and the wind can feel like a hairdryer in your throat. This was going to be uncomfortable! I had not mentioned to Lorna about my previous driving experience with Antonio, hoping it was just macho showing-off and that he would tone it down in the presence of Lorna. Wishful thinking! By the time we had been through the blind corners, plus the hairdryer air, when we arrived at the Olive Mill, Lorna was angry, and feeling quite travel sick too!

I looked at Lorna and quickly realised that things were not going to go well. "Are you okay?" I asked.

"Not really, no. Let's just get on with it." She was green around the gills and Antonio was oblivious to the discomfort he had caused.

Antonio was playing a harmonica badly and

serenading Caroline. Caroline was lapping it up and giggling like a schoolgirl, but we weren't being taken in by his patter. We did the tour. However, I was not feeling the enthusiasm I was hoping for from Lorna. Obviously Neil and Caroline picked up on this too, and they invited us back for lunch the following day – without Antonio. We agreed.

Back at the hotel Lorna was in the shower, and I called out to her. "You didn't like it, did you?" I asked.

"It's not that I don't like it, I do, but I just didn't get that feeling, you know. I wanted to love it, I really did. I can see that it could be a good investment, and it would change our life, but I wanted it to be perfect." She was despondent. She knew how much I loved the house, and she wanted to love it just as much. But she was happy to give it another go the following day, but was not by any means convinced.

The following morning we set off on our journey back to the Olive Mill, slightly nervous of getting lost in the countryside as this would be our first visit on our own. We took the drive slowly and appreciated the different houses and views along the way.

As we turned onto the track, Lorna said, "Please, drive slowly."

So we did. At one point we reached the crest of a hill, and the view stretched for miles and miles, all the way to the mountains in Jaen. Thousands of beautiful olive trees, on undulating hills for as far as the eye could see. That view still takes my breath away. With Lorna feeling much better, having arrived without a green tinge, she was back to her usual self, and with Neil and Caroline putting on a lovely, leisurely lunch, we were both able to fully appreciate the wonderful charms of the beautiful place. Lorna loved it nearly as much as I did.

Neil was the one who started the conversation after lunch, "So then Lorna, hmm, hmm, eek, what do you think?" There was a noticeable change in the atmosphere.

Despite our planned, not too enthusiastic approach, Lorna and I were all smiles and looked at each other and back at Neil, "We want to buy your house!" we said. We didn't make an offer or agree to go away and talk to the agent; we just agreed to pay the price there and then.

"The only thing is," I said, "We need to sell our house, although that shouldn't be a problem. Lorna has to work until Christmas, so we would want to complete the sale in the New Year. Oh, and one other thing…. How would you feel about leaving Mary-Belle behind?"

"Eek, well, to be honest, hmm, eek, that would be good, as she can be difficult to transport, hmm-eek." By now, with the excitement of the situation, the twitching and squeaking was off the chart.

We shook hands there and then and agreed to organise a deposit as soon as possible.

We instructed a solicitor in Spain to deal with the sale. In fact the solicitor we used was José, who I had met in Ronda. We then put the house in the UK up for sale, after weeks of preparation. We were confident of a quick sale, possibly within weeks.

Chapter 6
Crisis

"Oh shit!" I muttered, "Lorna, come and look. All these people are queuing up outside the building societies on the news, trying to get their money out. The news is saying there is some sort of banking crisis!"

"Oh, really? What does that mean?"

"Well, they are saying that they think this banking crisis could affect the housing market. It shouldn't be too much of a problem for us, though, this house should still sell."

As the weeks passed we had a few interested viewers but the expected offers didn't materialise. However we were still hopeful and confident things would be okay. We arranged to make another trip, in October, to see Neil and Caroline at the Olive Mill, and also see Peter and Penny at Ronda and discuss our alpaca requirements. We had given them a budget, and we were keen to see what they could come up with. This would also be the first chance for Chris and Frankie to see their future home.

Over the next few weeks we began to slowly tell people, friends and work colleagues of our plans for a new life. Many were shocked, particularly those who had known Lorna in a professional capacity, but without exception everyone wished us well.

When we explained the reasoning behind our decision to friends and family, we began to hear the phrases that were to become all too common to us, "You're so brave" or "I would so love to do something like that." It really annoys me when people say this to us. We are no different or any braver than anyone else, and I just want to say to them, "Go on then, just do it!" I truly believe we only live once, and I would hate to get to the end of my life and say that I had not tried something different, or that I was never brave enough. Well… WE WERE BRAVE ENOUGH!

So, now the people around us knew, and the deposit was paid on the Spanish house; we were fast approaching the point of no return.

As the October trip drew close, the day before we left, Chris suffered an epileptic fit and was unable to travel, so Chris and Frankie stayed in Brighton. This would mean they would miss their last chance to see the house before we moved to Spain. They would be moving to a whole new country, without even seeing the house they were due to live in. They had to trust us completely.

The first two days of the trip were spent at the Olive Mill with Neil and Caroline, and Neil talked us through some extra little bits of work he had done. We loved his 'rustic' style of work, and we discussed the possibility of using Neil for some work we had planned after we arrived. Of course he was very keen.

On the last night of the Montoro leg of our visit, we found out it was the annual local fair (*Feria*), and we decided to check it out. The *Feria* ground in Montoro is situated around the bullring, and there are fabulous lights erected every year, and a large fairground with rides in attendance. The ladies of the town wear their traditional gypsy dresses and the children wear the most adorable outfits. Most of the locals will attend the *Feria* every night, and eat, drink and dance flamenco until the 'wee small hours' and stumble home at around 6 in the morning to recover for the next night's celebrations.

The night we visited, there happened to be a parade of fire eaters and snake handlers, all accompanied by scantily clad dancers of both sexes. One of the male dancers was a particularly flamboyant, very camp, Cristiano Ronaldo lookalike. It was quite a spectacle, and made for a terrific atmosphere. We left at a decent hour as we had to drive to Ronda the next morning to discuss our alpacas, unlike the locals, who continued to party throughout the night!

We arrived at the *finca* of Peter and Penny in the early afternoon to be greeted like long-lost relatives. I endured an uncomfortable man-hug from Peter, as we said our hellos.

"This is Lorna," I said, and introduced her to the people who would change our life!

"So nice to meet you, luvvie," Penny exclaimed. "I've been looking forward to this for weeks, and we've got something for you!"

We were presented with a brochure, detailing the package of animals they were proposing to supply us. This consisted of four animals, one from the herd already in Spain (Bermuda had a fearsome reputation, mainly from putting a posturing Peter on his backside one time, but as such she came at a bargain price). We have since discovered that Bermuda is just a very nervous animal, and she has grown to trust us, far more than she ever could in a large herd. Three more were to arrive as part of a shipment of animals due out in Spain in January.

"Now, there is a spreadsheet here, showing the return you might be expected to make, if everything goes well," they said.

The piece of paper showed our four girls, breeding yearly and averaging two male and two female cria (baby alpacas) each year. The return after four years seemed fantastic, and would be about 200% of our initial investment. This would be enough for us to live on. The Olive Mill ran on solar power, therefore no electricity bills, and the water came from a spring. This meant our living costs would be significantly lower than in the UK. On top of that our council tax was about €180 for the year!

"Okay, this is good, but there are some things we are worried about. For a start, we have never done this before, we are complete beginners. How will we know what to do?" I asked nervously.

"Don't worry too much about all that. These animals are perfect for novices. They very rarely get ill, and all they need are some annual injections and their toe nails trimming a couple of times. They get sheared once a year, but we will organise that. Don't worry, we will be here every step of the way. I will even get in my smart car and drive up to your house as soon as I hear when a baby is on

28

its way." Penny replied enthusiastically.

"Okay, I think we are in!" I said. "Maybe we can sort the deposit out when we get back to the UK? How does that sound?"

"Perfect. That sounds just perfect. Congratulations and welcome to the alpaca club!" Peter beamed.

That evening Peter and Penny laid on a barbecue, for us to meet another couple who were also investing in alpacas. Tom and Lucy were a lovely couple and we got on well with them instantly. They got into alpacas because Lucy had a dream about owning these animals, and then they heard about Peter and Penny, and their alpaca business. Fate, I guess! We had a lovely evening under the stars, talking all things alpaca, and about the future for the industry in Andalucía, and Spain in general. We were positive we were making the correct decision, and we could be getting in at the start of something magical.

We went to bed knowing we had to rise early, to leave at five, to catch our flight at the airport. Peter insisted on getting up too, and even made breakfast, which was very welcome.

Peter pointed us in the right direction "Right, take the first track to the left, and then follow the track up to the road, and you should be fine. Just pick up the signs for Malaga."

"Okay, thanks Peter! See you soon." We waved as we drove off.

It was pitch black; there is no street lighting in rural Andalucia, so when I missed the turning on the track and continued on through a row of olive trees, it was a number of minutes before we realised something was wrong.

"Errrm, Alan, I think we are going the wrong way. I don't remember the track being this long and bumpy before!" Lorna looked at me.

"I'm not sure either. Damn!"

We turned around, but that seemed to confuse the issue even more. Everywhere we looked, all we could see were rows and rows of olive trees, all in perfect symmetrical lines in every direction.

"Oh my God, we're totally lost," said Lorna as we bumped our tiny hire car along between the olives. We stopped and got out of the car and looked around. We could make out one tiny light, so we headed off again in that direction, slowly, slowly, and after about five or six minutes we emerged from the olive grove, back on the track, only about 50 metres away from where Peter had waved us off. Thankfully at least no one had seen us. If we ever have visitors, I insist on meeting them, thus avoiding a repeat of this incident. Trying to find a tiny car, amidst kilometre upon kilometre of olive trees is no easy feat - the proverbial needle in a haystack.

Back in Brighton, we made our way back to the farm park, which had become our unofficial place to go for serious discussion and talk about our options. While we were there, we got talking to the farm manager and discussed our plans with him.

"The thing is," he said, "alpacas are expensive. Why don't you buy half a dozen non-breeding males, and for a year or two get used to them, holding them and handling them, and then if you still feel like breeding later, you will be more experienced. Plus, it will cost you much, much less."

This seemed a highly sensible option, and we vowed to discuss the situation seriously and also talk it over with Peter and Penny when we next spoke. A few days later Penny phoned to see how we were doing.

"Hi Penny, I'm glad you've phoned. There is something we wanted to discuss with you. We have been talking to a farm manager, local to us here, and he has suggested that maybe we should buy some cheap males, and just get used to having them and looking after them for a while before we decide to breed. We think the idea is quite good. What do you think?"

Penny was put out. "Well, to be quite honest Alan, I thought you wanted to do this properly. The best way to get into this business is to buy the best animals you can afford and breed them. A pregnant female costs the same to feed as a pet male. I have spent hours and hours putting together this package for you, calling in all sorts of favours and now there are people relying on my word! You can't let them all down now."

"Umm, no. That wasn't my intention, Penny, it was just a thought we had. Of course we wouldn't want to let anybody down, we will carry on as we promised."

Peter had been a good salesman, thorough and detailed, but that piece of subtle (ish) emotional blackmail clinched them the deal, and we agreed to continue with the original plan. Maybe, in hindsight, we should have been stronger!

The plans were coming together. We had secured a house in Spain and put a deposit down on some animals that would hopefully provide us with an adequate income for the future. We were beginning to get excited about our new life.

We had been advised (by books, Internet and know-it-alls), that we should be learning Spanish before we left. Luckily, at one of the schools where Lorna taught, there was a lovely half Greek, half native New York man who had lived in Madrid, and was the teacher of Spanish to the juniors. This was perfect, we felt we needed the basics. We were able to walk through our Spanish abc's and our basic numbers, and learn some important phrases like, "*Mas despacio, por favour*" which means 'more slowly please'. The Spanish have a tendency to combine all the words in a sentence into one long drawn-out word, without taking a breath, so it can be difficult to understand, especially where we were going to live. The lessons went okay: we managed to learn a little, but mainly we laughed a lot. The teacher was quite camp, obviously gay, and quite enjoyed getting us jigging about as though we were part of a Spanish fiesta, all the while practising our basics. When we got something right, we would all cry, "*¡Estupendo!*" It was a riot.

However, after we arrived in Spain we realised that the Andalucían accent is strong, and they 'eat' a lot of their letters and tend to not even pronounce the letter 's'. Ever! Throw on top of that, in the area where we live, the majority of people are farmers, many of whom cannot even read or write, and you will understand why three months of learning proper Spanish, with proper pronunciation, did not stand us in very good stead. We have since been told, in no uncertain terms by a local lady, that if we wanted to speak proper Spanish, we should have moved to Madrid.

Chapter 7
Into the Frying Pan

As the time of completion grew nearer, to save us the time and expense of travelling back and forth to sign paperwork, we decided to give our solicitor power of attorney to act on our behalf. So one day we boarded a train to London and set off for a meeting with a notary at the Spanish Embassy.

"How can I help you?" the lady at the Embassy greeted us.

"We have an appointment with the notary to organise power of attorney for our solicitor."

"Okay, wait here a moment."

We were then shown into a large office and asked to sit down and wait for a few minutes and the notary would be with us as soon as possible.

The notary came in and we told her of our plans. "We are buying a house in Cordoba, in Andalucía, and we need to organise power of attorney for our solicitor."

"Oooh, Cordoba. I love Cordoba, it's a beautiful city! I lived there for a while myself. Do you know that they call Cordoba the frying pan of Spain?"

"No, we have never heard that. Why?"

"It's because of the temperature. When I was living there, one day I remember the temperature reaching 50 degrees."

"50 degrees!" I nearly choked. "Oh my God, I don't even like sunbathing!"

Over the next few weeks we attended a variety of goodbye meals, parties and get-togethers. From meals with family members, parties at the dance school with three generations of families, and even a special leaving party that Frankie and Chris arranged for their friends.

We had decided that instead of a traditional leaving

party, filled with loud music and drunkenness, we wanted to have a day at the local farm park that had been such an inspiration to us. This gave many of our nearest and dearest the chance to get up close and personal with these animals that had enchanted and captivated us. Whilst I think the day was successful and fun, I think that a lot of our friends and family didn't really 'get it' and I think they still struggle with it to this day.

As we said goodbye to people that day, it was with a little trepidation; the day was drawing close and we would be starting our new life in less than 48 hours. We had said goodbye; 'i's were dotted and 't's had been crossed. This was going to be an adventure. A new life beckoned us all. This was, in every aspect, us going 'Into the Frying Pan'.

Chapter 8
Goodbye Grey Sky

Official moving day was 16th January 2008, and the taxi for the airport was booked for 4 am. We had managed to secure flights where we each had a luggage allowance of 30kg, so we were able to get as much as possible into our cases for our first few weeks. Our relatively small amount of belongings would be with us in about 14 days. Geri the dog was also able to be accommodated and we only had to pay the cost of her weight as excess baggage. This saved a great deal of money on the prices we were quoted by animal travel agencies.

So, after waking at 3 am, although I don't remember getting much sleep at all, we were packing various necessities for the first few days. One plastic plate each, knives and forks, plastic cups and plenty of clothes. The plan was, when we arrived, we would go shopping at the supermarket and pick up a couple of cooking pots and some bedding, pillows and duvets. Neil and Caroline had kindly left two beds for us to use until our furniture arrived. We shoved Geri (literally) in to her (very large) box and loaded the taxi, said goodbye to relatives who had turned out in their pyjamas to say goodbye, and away we went. At this point it felt as though we were going on a long holiday, we just didn't know when we would be returning. Chris and Frankie had never even seen the house, so I can only imagine how they must have been feeling!

Having arrived at the airport, we checked in our baggage, and found out what we needed to do with Geri. We had to take her to the cargo desk, next to the security queues, and present her newly- acquired (and expensive) passport and travel documents.

Lorna said goodbye to Geri through the door of her

crate and we started to walk down to the security gate.

"Oh dear, listen to that," Lorna said with a grimace. Geri was crying. Loudly.

As we walked towards security, the crying got louder and louder. "Oh no, I hope she is going to be okay."

"I'm sure she will be fine once she's loaded and there's no one around. She's just attention seeking." I tried to assure Lorna, but I wasn't sure. I just hoped all would be fine. As we walked up to security, it felt as though the eyes of the terminal were upon us. Who knows how long, or how loud she cried?

For the first time I think reality began to set in for us all while we waited to board that plane. We were really moving! Abroad! To rural Spain! To breed alpacas! What were we thinking?

Chapter 9
Hello Blue

Animal count: One dog, one feral cat, one pot bellied pig
(Mary-Belle came with the house, as agreed)

We landed in our new home, sunny Spain, at Malaga airport at around 9 am. Frankie, eager to see outside, was disappointed.

"It's bloody raining. Would you believe it, we move to Spain, and it's just like England, grey and drizzly."

"I'm sure there will be plenty of sunny days, Frankie," Lorna assured her.

We queued up through passport control, and went to wait for our baggage. We had been told that once we had collected our luggage we could collect Geri from the cargo collection area.

"Okay, now we've got the bags, where do we find Geri?" Lorna was looking around anxiously.

"I think there's a cargo collection point down there," I said pointing to the end of the terminal.

"Shhh, listen," Frankie said suddenly. "Can you hear crying? Like Geri was before?"

We all listened carefully. We could all hear it, and it was getting louder.

"There!" Chris cried, pointing towards the rubber curtain at the end of the luggage conveyor belt.

Sure enough, there, emerging from the tunnel, was Geri's container. There was much laughter and looking at her, as she circled the carousel, crying like a banshee. She also smelled pretty bad too, having been caught short in her crate. We lifted her off the carousel, and onto a trolley. We couldn't believe there was no paperwork to do or anything; the Spanish baggage handlers had just put her out with the luggage. Although I am not sure how much she enjoyed the travelling, I would like to think it was worth it, as she is now able to enjoy her Spanish retirement home.

Now that we had everything, there were formalities and business to attend to. We picked up a large people carrier which we had hired for three weeks, enough to give us time to settle in, and, we hoped, find a second-hand car to buy. We were due to meet Sarah, the estate agent, en route to our appointment at the notary to complete the purchase. Our solicitor, José, was also to meet us there.

I was feeling slightly nervous, as Neil and Caroline had been in touch with us in the days before we moved, asking us to bring a large amount of cash out as part of the purchase. We had heard that a lot of purchases were done in this way, which included handing over 'black money', as it meant only declaring a certain amount of the purchase price and avoiding some of the tax. Even the notaries are in on the act, and they leave the room for this part of proceedings. José had, however, assured me that he would deal with the financials, so I was under the impression that maybe he would have this cash on him, drawn from our house purchase account.

At the notary's office, we met up with Neil, Caroline and their solicitors, Antonio and José. I managed to have a quiet word with José about my concerns, but he said an abrupt 'No', that we were to complete the purchase in the legal way, and declare the total cost. This would be better for us in the long run. I must admit to breathing a sigh of relief as José seemed to be on top of things.

We were ushered in to a room with a large conference table, and the notary entered. It was a little bit as though a priest or a judge was in the room; the solicitors seemed a little in awe of the man. I guess they are men of power. There was much shushing and looks of 'be quiet'.

We were taken through the house paperwork, and it was translated for us, and then the financial side of things came around. Things became slightly uncomfortable here, as Caroline was particularly upset that there was no cash to be handed over. They were planning on paying their commissions to the estate agents using that cash. So Caroline proceeded to phone her bank in the middle of the notary's office, trying to arrange to collect funds later in the day. There were dagger looks from both solicitors and the notary, but Caroline was oblivious. At one point she even raised her hand to her solicitor who was trying to get her to end the call. It seemed hugely disrespectful, and left a slightly sour taste. It could have been dealt with after.

Once formalities were complete, there was much handshaking and cheek kissing, twice of course, and keys were handed over.

Outside the office, we talked to Neil and Caroline.

"Errmm, eekk, we do have a little bad news I'm afraid, hmm eek. We haven't been able to arrange the removals van for today, so we need to come and collect everything tomorrow. We hope that's okay with you, eek eek."

Caroline added, "And, the dogs are there for tonight, and the horses can't be collected until the weekend because of paperwork! We will be up tomorrow to collect the dogs, and show you how to feed the horses for a few days. Don't worry, it will be fine!"

"Errr, okay," was all I could muster. We had no real choice but to go with it, our furniture and belongings were not due to arrive for a couple of weeks anyway. With that we headed up the motorway towards Cordoba.

When we first pulled off the motorway and started heading into the countryside, the nerves began to tell!

"Is this it? How much further? Are we there yet?" Chris and Frankie kept asking.

But then we turned off the road onto the dirt track for the final section of the journey. They must have been exhausted, nervous, excited and very wary, all rolled into one. We took the track slowly, as Geri was still in her travelling crate, and the hire car was brand new, and we didn't want to damage it.

As we pulled up outside the house Lorna announced, "Now, this is it, this is our new home."

"Wow, it's massive, it's like a castle!" was Frankie's

first reaction. Chris's was more, "Oh my God, it really is in the middle of nowhere!"

With the horses still at the house and the peaceful setting it was like arriving at a tranquil rural holiday destination. (I must admit, some days we wake up and it still feels like a holiday, even four years down the line.) We unloaded the car and let Geri out for a drink and a wee, and showed the kids around.

"Right it's going to get dark soon," I said. "Your mum and I need to get to the supermarket, to buy some stuff for the beds and a bit of food. Let's get the fire lit, and we can let you two relax and find your feet a bit!"

"Good idea," said Lorna.

In January much as in the UK, the days are short and it gets dark before six. Once the sun goes down, especially in the winter, it also gets cold. This is something most people in the UK just don't realise. They think it is always sunshine and hot, but in the winter the weather can be incredibly cold, there is even frost and ice on the cars in the morning.

We also still needed to get to the supermarket to buy some food and some bedding for that night, as although we had brought some bed linen with us, we had no pillows or duvets. Chris and I gathered some firewood from a pile left behind, and Neil had kindly left a box of firelighters, so we lit a fire. Lorna and I headed back out, up the track, and left Frankie and Chris to relax for a while. We headed out to find a supermarket we had been told was only 30 minutes away, and it was already about 7.30 pm.

We took the track back up to the motorway, driving a little slower now, as it was dark, and we headed on the motorway in the direction of a town called Andujar, home to a large supermarket where you can buy practically everything. When we reached Andujar, we could see the signs for the supermarket but we missed the turning, took the next one instead and ended up driving around a country track for what seemed like an age.

We eventually made it back to the motorway and arrived at the supermarket at about 9.30 pm. It closed at 10 pm. We rushed around buying only the essentials, pillows of funny shapes and very thin duvets. We managed to pick up a few snacky foods to get us through the evening and headed back home. By the time we arrived back, at about 11 pm, we were exhausted. We walked into the apartment, hoping at least Frankie and Chris had been able to relax.

"Hi you two, are you okay?" The apartment was freezing cold.

"Erm, no, not really," was Frankie's unhappy reply.

Chris took over, "The problem is, we couldn't get the fire going. When you left, it looked fine, but that was just the firelighters. I've gone through a whole box of firelighters and it's still not going! All it's doing is smoking a bit."

"And it's bloody freezing," Frankie added. "We had to huddle together on this chair and get Geri on our laps to keep us warm."

"Oh my God," Lorna said sadly. "I'm so sorry, we thought it would be good for you two to have some time on your own, maybe you should have come with us. Maybe we should just all go to bed now, it's been a long day and we're all exhausted. At least we will be warm in bed."

I think if we had given them the option, both Chris and Frankie (and Geri) would have caught the first available flight home.

The following day we awoke to beautiful blue skies, and for the next three weeks, 21 one full days, we hardly saw a cloud in the sky. This kind of winter weather was the reason we had moved to Spain, we were sick of grey!

We congregated in the living room to find that none of us had slept very well: the beds that had been left behind 'generously' by Neil and Caroline were very uncomfortable, and although we had been warned that it would be cold at night, it was much, much colder than we had imagined. Thick stone walls, tiled floors and a lack of central heating take some getting used to, and we were going to need much more than just one night. In actual fact, a week or so later, we even found a pane of glass missing in the living room, that we hadn't even noticed. No wonder it felt so cold!

Neil and Caroline were due first thing in the morning to collect their furniture, dogs and to show us how to look after the horses for a few days, so we were up and about early. Neil brought up a horse-box that he had packed with some hay, and he loaded some small pieces of furniture. He then proceeded to load two ducks in one box, six chickens in another box, three cats in baskets and six loose dogs, all in this horse box together. The last one to be loaded was 'Bailey' the big Spanish Mastiff.

"In you go big fella, eek, hmmm!"

He was hurled in with a startled expression on his face, and the door was shut quickly before he could recover and get over his initial shock. Who knows what the police would have made of it if they had pulled them over and decided to check the horse-box. Once the furniture was loaded onto the removal van and everything was on its way, we were alone for a few days. The horses would be collected at the weekend.

We decided we needed to get some food for a few days so we headed in to Montoro to do some shopping. We had heard that the girl in the local bakers liked to try and speak a little English, so we headed there first.

"*Hola, beunas dias,*" we proudly said and started pointing and looking at the cakes and bread.

Luckily we had found the right girl, and she started to talk to us in broken English.

"You are Engleeesh, si?"

"Yes, yes we are. We have just bought a house here."

"*Ah si, claro.* You leeve in Montoro?" She asked us in very slow and considered English.

"Yes. Well, in the countryside, just outside," I replied.

With that there was some chatter from behind us, and we had been surrounded by a crowd of people around us, marvelling at the new English people and talking to us in Spanish that we had no chance of understanding, being spoken at 100 miles an hour. It was quite a daunting situation but strangely welcoming at the same time. There were lots of smiles and back-slapping going on. We didn't really understand much that day, and that has never happened since, so maybe it was some kind of strange welcoming procedure, who knows?

Sometime later, we did hear from a friend of ours who lives in the town, that when she first moved here, some of the older ladies would touch her hair, to try and see if they could see the roots as she was blonde. These strange invasions of privacy are very common here. People, even men, are very touchy-feely, and it is not unknown, if you have a baby, for a Spanish lady to just come up and take the baby out of the pushchair and talk to it and cuddle it without even asking you.

I didn't really know what was going on for a long time before we moved to our new house. I was ferried back and forth to the vets (my least favourite place on earth), where they stuck me with needles, took my blood and gave me pills. They even took a photo of me looking daft, and stuck it in a book. Apparently this was all necessary. I tried to put up a fight, but those floors they have in the vets, I can never get a grip to hold on, and they always get me in there in the end.

The day we left our old house, I didn't know what to make of it. They had emptied the house, and in the middle of the night I was woken abruptly, shoved in a container, and loaded into a car. After a while I settled down, but then they left me with some strange men, at a very large place. I tried to call them to come back, I was hungry, but they didn't listen.

The men loaded me onto a large vehicle and then it all went dark and very loud. I was thirsty and hungry and desperate for the toilet. In the end I just had to go in that box, it was very unpleasant. When they lifted me out of the darkness, it was very warm. Suddenly I was moving, but I could hear the voices of my people, so I started to shout to them again. This time they came for me, I could see them all coming towards me, I was so happy. They put me into a

43

new car, and we drove for a while, but when we got out, it wasn't our normal house, it was somewhere new. It smells strange, but there are lots of trees, and lots of places to lie out in the sun. I think I am going to like it here.

Geri

Chapter 10
Beautiful Girls

A couple of days into our adventure, and with aching backs and legs from sleeping in the cold, and on the world's most uncomfortable beds, we made our way down to Ronda. Peter and Penny were due to be receiving their new shipment of animals over from the UK, and it included three of the animals that we were buying. We thought this would be an ideal opportunity to catch up with them and also introduce Frankie and Chris to the people and the animals that were going to have such an impact on all our lives.

We arrived at the top of the track at the house in Ronda to find a big gathering of expectant expats, and a few curious locals, although they tended to be standing back watching from afar. They were all here to see the arrival of these strange looking animals. The reason everybody was waiting at the top of the track was because the transporter was too large to make it all the way down to the house. It was going to need to unload ten animals at a time at the top and reload them onto Peter's trailer, and then they would be ferried down to the fields.

When the transporter arrived, there was a noticeable buzz of anticipation in the air. The back of the lorry was opened and everybody took turns to clamber up and have a look in. The vast majority of the 30 or so animals on board were white, as this was the breeder's preference, but there were about three or four Alpacas that were coloured, and two of our beautiful girls stood out a mile. Black Dancer was obviously black, and Cassandra, a beautiful brown, and they were both lovely looking animals. Cassandra is always cooed over by non-alpaca visitors. (She is not the most perfect alpaca in a competitive sense, but she has lovely eyes and eyelashes, and people tend to notice this).

Our lovely white girl Lily was also on board.

We had decided we would choose two animals of different colours to try and provide something a little bit different to what was already being bred in the area, and hopefully if another breeder had a client who was maybe looking for a coloured animal, we might be able to work together. Sadly, it didn't quite work out like we hoped in that respect.

One of the first questions we are always asked when we meet someone new is 'Why alpacas?' So I thought it would be a good opportunity to give a little background on the animals, to help you understand our (crazy) decision.

Alpacas come in a range of 22 natural colours, from white, through fawn, to brown, and also grey and black colours. Throughout Europe, alpaca breeding is still relatively unknown. However there is an industry built up around it that includes clothing (alpaca fleece has no lanolin, and is therefore hypoallergenic, and is considered to be of equivalent quality to cashmere), bedding, selling the animals as pets and chicken guards, and selling show quality animals to be used to compete in competitions and win prizes.

Obviously the better animals you have to breed with, the better quality the offspring, and therefore the price you can command for sale. The real reason alpacas exist is because of the quality of the fleece, but most farms make money by producing the best animals they can, and selling them on to new breeders. In 2010, there was one stud male, in the US, which sold for $675,000. One animal! So, apart from falling in love with the animals themselves, we wanted a little slice of this action, and Peter and Penny's enthusiasm was contagious. Our two coloured girls which had come from the UK were both bred to top males, and they were due to be delivered to us first, in April. The two white girls would be delivered later, as Bermuda was heavily pregnant and Lily needed to be mated. Our first babies were due in the summer.

We had a lovely day at the farm, with lots of food and drink, lots of new people to meet and lots of highly motivating alpaca talk. We really felt as though we were at the start of something big, and felt proud to be part of this pioneering group. We left that day with a real sense of excitement and anticipation, keen to get started on cleaning up the paddocks as soon as the horses were moved at the weekend.

Chapter 11
Alone at Last

After a week of horse-sitting we were ready for them to be collected, so we could get our new lives started properly. Neil and Caroline were due to meet the Spanish horse-transport man at a local garage, and then bring him to the house. When they arrived, the man was typically Andalucían; weather-beaten, wearing a flat cap, with a cigarette hanging from his mouth. He spoke in a series of grunts and shrugs.

The first two or three horses were loaded without an issue, but when they tried to load the large mare into the lorry, she was not happy. She reared and bucked, and the driver fell into the wall and cracked his head open. He was shaken up quite badly. This mare really didn't want to go in. Neil tried, but the horse was no calmer; The Horse Whisperer he certainly wasn't. She was snorting and breathing heavily, whilst Neil was squeaking and twitching with all the stress. It was a real sight to behold, and of course not the usual sight we would have seen in Brighton on a Saturday morning. Eventually the horse calmed down, and she walked into the lorry of her own accord to be with her friends. She just needed a bit of patience and time.

Once the animals were out of the way we decided to crack on with cleaning the paddocks in preparation for the arrival of our beautiful girls. We thought it would take a few hours to clear all the horse manure but we had underestimated the situation, and four days later we cleared the last wheelbarrow-full. We had moved about 12 solid inches of manure from two paddocks that were completely buried. We came to the conclusion that those animals had never been cleaned out in the time they had lived there, as we never found any piles of cleared manure anywhere.

During this period of impetus, Lorna and Frankie also threw themselves into the manual labour side of things to enable us to get as much done as possible, in as short a time as possible. Of course being English and with the sun shining, we were all in shorts and T-shirts, and Frankie was working in the manure, wearing an ensemble of wellington boots, hot pants, strappy top and gardening gloves. At one point a car full of Romanian olive workers drove past her working, and very nearly drove straight off the track. In all the years they had been working here they would be used to seeing the older Spanish women wearing their dinner-lady tabards or their bright pink housecoat and slippers. So to see an 18-year-old dancer in her hot pants must have come as a welcome change. I'm sure she also quite liked the attention!

Frankie also had one of her first encounters with the local wildlife, as she found a family of tiny field mice in the manure, which she tried to re-home in the new pile, but of course they all shot off as soon as she came near them.

Once the paddocks were clean, we had to try to obtain a licence, to enable us to move the animals from Ronda to our house. We had heard that getting these licences could be a bit difficult, as some people had been told they needed zoo or exotic animal licences. We armed ourselves with photos of cute baby alpacas, and headed to the local offices of OCA (the Spanish version of Defra), and tried to speak to the girls behind the reception desk. We showed them the photos of the alpacas, and said simply, "*Perdon, Ingles.*" (This was about the extent of our Spanish for months, if not years.) One of the girls spoke a (very) little English but she said she had called the head '*veterinario*' and we were to wait here.

A stern-faced woman in her mid-30s appeared from an office, and made her way towards us. She, happily, did speak a little English and we were able to explain that we had moved to the area and would like to keep some alpacas at our house. We showed our pictures and she

49

explained to the girls behind the desk about the photos and what alpacas were. There was much "oohing" and "aahing" over the photos, and they didn't seem to believe these animals would be living in Montoro. After that we felt that they were on our side; the vet said she would look into it for us, if we could wait for a few minutes.

"Sit down, Alan," she said sternly.

I don't think it was meant to come across as though I was being told off, but I felt suitably chastised. It was just the Spanish way of speaking. They were, in actual fact, very helpful, and we were told that all we needed to do, was speak to the local vet, who would come to our house and see if it was suitable for alpacas, and then draw up a plan to submit to OCA for the licence. As there had been horses there before, they didn't think we would have any issues. This meant the next port of call was the town vet.

We visited Manuel, the vet, who we had been told had a good grasp of English. We had heard correctly: his English was much better than our Spanish was, and still is now, in fact.

"Manuel, we would like to bring some animals here, to Montoro, to breed them and keep them at our house in the countryside. They are called alpacas!"

"Alpacas? I don't understand. Alpacas are food for horses? No?"

Okay, so his English wasn't that good. But we did manage to establish that alpacas in Spanish means 'bales of hay'. We have become proficient in explaining that alpacas are similar to llamas (pronounced yammas!).

We were able to ask firstly, if he would come to our house to do the OCA paperwork, and secondly, would he be happy to be our vet and treat the alpacas if we needed him. We explained what little we knew, including how healthy and hardy alpacas as a species are. Of course he had never seen an alpaca, but he said he would be happy to have us as clients, and he would do a little research in the meantime. The only problem was (and is), although Manuel is an emergency vet, he does not drive, so we have to go and collect him from the town, which does involve a one-hour round trip. One of the downsides of living so far in the countryside, I guess!

The three weeks with our lovely hire car came to an end quickly, and we made the rash decision to go out on the day we needed to return the hire car, and try to buy ourselves a car there and then. Looking back now, we should have hired a car for another couple of weeks and we would have been able to look around in a more relaxed manner.

Neil had offered to show us around a few places he knew of, where there were second-hand cars available, so he met us at Malaga airport (a three-hour drive) and off we went. We were looking for an automatic, Spanish 4x4, the thinking being it would be easier for Lorna to get used to driving an automatic. It also needed to be a reasonable price. Cars in Spain don't seem to depreciate in value in the same way they do in the UK, so even cars a few years old, and with miles on the clock, can be pricey.

After visiting a few garages with no luck, Neil phoned an ad he had seen in the local English free paper and spoke to guy named Alex, selling an English 4x4, but automatic. It sounded positive so we headed off to have a look. The car seemed in good order. We had a test drive and Alex seemed like a genuine guy, so we decided to go for it. The price was €4,500 and seeing us for the suckers we were, he held out for the full price, seemingly aware of the situation we had put ourselves in. It was a rookie mistake to admit that we needed the car that day, and probably cost us a few hundred euros (much more in the long run, as you will see). We were told we would need someone to sort out the ownership paperwork for us, but that shouldn't be a problem. We were delighted to have secured some transport for ourselves.

We headed off home, reasonably pleased with ourselves and with one more thing crossed off the 'to do' list.

Chapter 12
Miguel, Fires and Giraffes

One morning over the next few days, we were all out in the 'grounds' doing some weeding. A man came by on a tractor, and introduced himself to us as Miguel, the neighbour from up the hill, the owner of our house previous to Neil and Caroline and the farmer of the olives.

Miguel is about mid-50s, with a slightly less weathered face than most Andalucíans, maybe because of his love of a straw hat, with lots of hair in a shade somewhere between white and grey, thick glasses and a very smiley disposition. We swapped telephone numbers, although I am not entirely sure how he thought we would communicate on the telephone, and he said basically if we ever needed him, to shout up to his house when he was there and he would come and see us. This was explained by Miguel putting his hands to the side of his mouth and yelling "Miguel!". He then managed to make it understood that he would come over to our house tomorrow, with his wife, Olga, who speaks English and they would have a drink with us.

The next evening, Miguel, Olga and their daughter Andrea arrived and they came in and made themselves comfortable (it had of course been their house previously). Olga was slightly younger than Miguel, maybe in her 40s, with shoulder-length blonde hair, very plain, and ever so slightly dumpy in her appearance. She was of course, a farmer's wife and as such was expected to work, so she couldn't be glammed up all the time. Andrea, the daughter, was like a miniature version of her mother, and very shy, especially in front of us, the strange foreigners.

The subject quickly turned to our olive trees, 360 to be precise, planted on very steep hills. It had never been our intention to farm these trees ourselves, so when Miguel suggested that he could carry on working the olives for us, as he had done for Neil and Caroline, and he would, in return, supply us with '*leňa*' for our '*fuego*' and '*mucho aciete*'. This was basically wood for our fire and as much oil as we would want. We accepted without hesitation. To be honest, if we could have sorted someone to work the olives for us, we probably could earn a little money from them, but at the time it was a weight off our mind, and meant we didn't have to worry about keeping the weeds and trees in check.

Once drinks were finished, we were ushered out and they insisted we accompany them up to their house for a drink. The women (and Chris) got in our car and headed up the hill while I was left to walk up with Miguel. I must admit he put me to shame, and by the time we reached the house, I was puffing and sweating, whereas Miguel was fresh as a daisy.

We were shown in through the front door, only to find that about a third of the house was a large open warehouse. There were onions and potatoes on the floor, picked from a vegetable patch somewhere, motorbikes in various stages of repair, a tractor, and every conceivable piece of pipe and tubing you could ever need. Spanish farmers have a reputation for never throwing anything away, it will always become useful.

Some steps took you up to the first floor level, with some very basic bedrooms and a bathroom, obviously prepared for the olive pickers when the time comes. On the ground floor, there was a large open space with a kitchen at one end, and a fireplace in the middle. There was not much furniture to speak of, just about eight plastic patio chairs and a couple of small tables situated around the fire.

Miguel took me proudly over to an unusual unmarked container with a tap on the outside and said proudly, "Vino". I had to try and explain that I don't drink alcohol, which they all seemed to find extremely funny; to them I was a man who only drinks Coca Cola, no beer and definitely no 'Whikky' as they pronounce whiskey. Lorna,

Frankie and Chris all tried the wine, and can testify to its potency. Our host was not one to let a glass run dry either, whenever a glass got put down or half emptied it was refilled.

Olga, who, it turned out, didn't speak English, but did own a dictionary and could read, provided us with some food to accompany our drinks. In my memory the food consisted of stale bread, crisps, miniature prawns, slimy peppers and some sort of pork scratching/pig fat concoction. Sadly, egg and chips it wasn't.

As the wine flowed, we managed to get onto the subject of horses. Miguel had heard that we were going to be having animals, I guess Neil and Caroline had been talking to him. We were, however, having a problem, as when he was talking about the alpacas he seemed to be making gestures that he thought that they were very large animals. We were having a problem at this stage with our communication, but Andrea actually managed to help us out. She drew a picture, of what we eventually deciphered to be a giraffe. Miguel and his family genuinely believed we were going to be breeding giraffes in the middle of the olive groves, but the thing is they didn't seem to think this was strange. They had just accepted it as part and parcel of the 'crazy English people'. We managed to clear up the situation as we had learnt a few words about alpacas and llamas. I have never quite got over the thought of a herd of giraffes bounding through our land. It sounds amazing to me.

As the wine was flowing, the conversations were becoming more and more animated. Miguel had some horses and he wanted to know if we were planning to have any, or if indeed we had done any riding. This was communicated by an inebriated Miguel pretending to be on the back of a horse, and jumping about. We all said we hadn't, but by this time Miguel's focus was on Chris. Miguel said he would take Chris out riding. Chris tried to explain that he was epileptic (*'epileptico'*), so probably shouldn't be on a horse. Well, the thought of Chris having an epileptic fit whilst riding a horse seemed to inspire

Miguel to new heights, and we were treated to an impersonation of Chris riding a horse and having an epileptic fit at the same time, all being performed by an aging, drunk Spanish farmer! It was, all in all, quite an eye-opening evening. We left, having been instructed that Chris and I would be out at 8 am, to collect some firewood with Miguel, for our fire in the house. It seemed fair to us, we needed the wood so we could help collect it.

At 8 am the following morning we made our way out to meet Miguel. We were a little nervous as talking and understanding was proving to be a little difficult. Miguel sat on his tractor and made a gesture that we should follow behind, and throw the wood in the trailer as we went. There were logs lying around from the trees that had been trimmed the previous year. That seemed pretty easy, we thought.

Around the trees at the lower end of the slopes, it was quite simple to negotiate our way around the hills, but as we cleared those logs Miguel told us to hold on to the back of the trailer and we headed up an enormously steep path, basically just being dragged along by the tractor. We were losing our footing, and getting cut to ribbons, dressed in our shorts, t-shirts, and completely unsuitable shoes. We were both wearing trainers more akin to wandering around the town centre shops rather than working the land. Both of our legs were cut, with blood trickling, and sweat was beginning to pour from us. Miguel of course was finding the whole situation hilarious, us city boys working. *"Mucho trabajo"* was the mantra for the day, of course interspersed with occasional re-enactments of his epileptic horse-riding impersonation. It did at least make the time pass quickly.

We stopped at an area where the trees had been trimmed but the branches had been left to dry, so they needed to be burned and the logs collected. We began to pile the branches up and Miguel used a lighter to ignite the pile… "Whooosh!" The branches went up in a myriad of flames about five metres high. I had never seen anything like it, every time another branch went on, "whoosh" again. It must be the oil in the branches, it burns very quickly and is very hot. Working underneath these fires, and of course with Miguel, did prove to be slightly hazardous. At the first fire, in one of the "whooshes" Miguel set light to his shirt, and leapt about dancing like a tribal warrior until he put it out! We were reduced to trying to avoid the burning embers that were falling from the sky, like some kind of scalding snowflakes. One of these embers must have landed on Miguel's straw hat, as the next thing we know, there is a 'yelp' and all we see is a straw hat rolling past, being blown along in the wind, but with the brim completely ablaze.

On one of the last fires, Miguel even managed to set alight to an olive tree. Being new to the area, and having heard about wildfires, I was a little alarmed by this, but Miguel was calm, poured some water on the tree and packed it with earth and soil and left it to burn out. A regular occurrence I would have to assume from the calm and considered manner in which it was dealt with!

After unloading the logs at the Olive Mill, Miguel trundled off on his merry way, back up the hill to his house. Chris and I collapsed in a heap, knowing we had done little for the reputation of the namby-pamby English amongst the Andalucían farming community. At least we had wood and we would be warm for the rest of the winter.

Chapter 13
The First Hiccup

The day before Valentine's Day, Chris and I announced to Lorna and Frankie that we were off out to collect some wood in the car for the fire and we set off on our 'secret' mission.

Once out on the track I said to Chris, "Right, the plan is, we bomb it into Montoro, look for some flowers and chocolates for the girls and get back here as quick as possible so they don't think we have been out too long."

"Okay, let's do it!" Chris replied.

Fifteen minutes down the road, as we approached the turn-off for Montoro, the temperature gauge in the car shot up and the car died.

"Oh shit, the car's just died. All the powers gone, even the steering!" I managed to coast on to the slip road, and pull off the road with the hazard lights on. "Shit, bugger and bloody hell. We've only had the thing a week!" We lifted the bonnet and there was steam, and lots of it. The only person we knew in town was Antonio, so I called him up.

"Hi Antonio, we need your help. Our car has just died on the roundabout coming into Montoro, and we don't know what to do."

"Alan. Hi. Okay. No worries, I can help. I know a man. Have you got a triangle? And yellow vests? No? Okay, get some, just in case the Guardia Civil come? It's the law. I'll send my friend down. Rodrigo from the garage. Sit tight. Adios."

Chris set off up the hill to the garage to buy a triangle and some yellow vests. As luck would have it, five minutes after he returned and we had placed the triangle down the road, the local Guardia Civil turned up. (The Guardia Civil are a branch of the Spanish army, and they deal with traffic policing and other important matters. They generally carry some sort of big scary firearm with them). The two that spoke to us did not speak any English, and once they had satisfied themselves that we were okay and not causing a problem, they just left us there and drove off.

When Rodrigo turned up, he opened the radiator cap and steam shot upwards like a geyser. He gave the mechanic's headshake that is understandable in any language, accompanied by enthusiastic teeth sucking; this is bad! After the engine cooled, and we put some water in, we were able to crawl back to Rodrigo's garage slowly through the streets of Montoro.

We had to call Lorna and Frankie, and own up to our plan, and explain that we were not sure how or when we were going to get home. At the garage, Rodrigo had a bit of a look at the car and seemed to be saying there was a problem, and it would cost around €2,000 to fix it. We had only had the car a week and didn't want to agree to anything too quickly. Our main priority had to be getting home that night. Maybe we could deal with it in the morning.

We tried to ask Rodrigo to phone us a taxi, and he said it would be an hour, as there was only one taxi in Montoro. While we were waiting, we had the pleasure of a visit from Antonio to see what was going on. He pulled up in his latest new car, a baby blue second-hand Porsche. Oh dear. The man just got worse. In the car with him was an attractive young girl, maybe 25 years his junior, who was very quiet and didn't seem to be able to speak very much. Rodrigo was nudging us and winking and laughing and saying, "Puta, puta" which we didn't understand. But he was laughing a lot with his young friend in the garage. Antonio didn't look happy and he went off with a scowl on his face.

After more than an hour of trying to talk to Rodrigo and his young friend, mainly about the universal language of football, a taxi had not arrived and it was starting to get dark. Another of Rodrigo's friends had arrived in a new-looking Audi, and we somehow managed to persuade him to take us home for €20. He was very happy to help us, and we were very grateful.

When we arrived home, after about three hours and without any Valentines' gifts, we felt a little disheartened. We looked up the word 'Puta' and found to our surprise that basically it means whore! We laughed as we finally got the joke.

I telephoned Alex, the English guy who we had bought the car from and he basically told us it was our problem; there wasn't anything he could do, as the car was fine when he sold it to us. I had always thought that English people living in a foreign country would stick together and help each other, but this was the first example of someone ripping off a fellow countryman that we came across, and sadly it wouldn't be the last.

Antonio gave us the number of Keith, an English guy who lived in Montoro, who had been a motorbike mechanic in the UK, and had moved to Spain after a bad accident as the weather helped his mobility. We arranged for Keith to collect us the following morning, and he offered to take us into town so we could do some shopping and he would have a look at the car for us. Keith knew some of the local mechanics so he said he would speak to a few for us, which we said would be great, but we would be without a car for a week or so. Keith offered to pick us up the following week to do another shop.

It just so happened that this period coincided with our first experience of bad Spanish weather, three weeks of cloudy grey skies and rain. This of course meant not a lot of solar power, and having no car, we had no means of getting out and buying petrol to enable us to run the back-up generator. We resorted to playing monopoly and scrabble by candlelight in the evenings, which is okay for one or two days but can get rather boring after a while. Plus, the rain also meant that we were unable to do any work during the day, so we had to read the few books we had, or play yet more board games. I think this period was hard for Frankie and Chris, as when the idea had been discussed we were all full of hope, optimism and ideas. However, we were still yet to sell the house in the UK, so our hands were tied and we were unable to spend much money until that happened.

After a week, Keith collected us again and said that he had spoken to a couple of garages who would look at our car, but it would take a week or two, and then we could get a proper diagnosis. Luckily, for the first three weeks of being carless Keith proved to be a real Good Samaritan for us, and never took any money for petrol.

During those three weeks also, I think Frankie and Chris started to miss their home comforts, at first the hand-washing had been a novelty but that was wearing off, and if she was feeling stressed, Frankie would take herself off to sit with Mary-Belle, and think. We knew it would be hard to adjust to life here, but this was our first testing period. We had never really discussed how it would be if things went wrong; I'm not sure that is something people want to envisage when embarking on a new part of their life. The first three weeks of living with our new solar electricity had been okay: we had had sunshine, and once our things arrived, we could watch TV in the evenings. But those weeks when we didn't have sun, and no petrol, we were reduced to never leaving a light on, reading by candlelight and going to bed early because we couldn't do anything else.

These days, we love our 'off-grid' lifestyle, but people often wonder how we manage. We have a washing machine, which we can use if it's sunny, and fridges, and these days we watch far less TV, maybe two hours in the evenings in the winter, probably not even that in the summer. If we have a period of time where there is no sun, we may not be able to do any washing for a week or two, but to be honest, do your clothes need to be washed after wearing them for a couple of hours? Probably not! We turn every appliance off at the mains when it is not being used, and we make the most of the available low wattage light bulbs. Our oven is gas, and we use an old fashioned kettle that sits on the hob. Our boilers also run from bottled gas.

We have become avid readers, and we work on the land in the mornings and evenings before and after the hottest part of the day, and in the real height of summer we 'siesta' like the natives. It's a great feeling to know that all our energy comes from the sun, and our water comes from a spring in the hill.

On the third week of our enforced imprisonment, when Keith collected us, we decided to all go into town, and we decided that the best course of action would be for me to catch a bus to Cordoba, and then a train to Malaga, to hire a car for a couple of weeks. Of course we looked into hiring a car closer to home, but the prices were astronomical. Obviously nothing was happening quickly with our car, and Lorna's son Mark and his partner were coming out to visit the following week, so we needed transport.

Being in a hurry to get back to Montoro to collect everyone, I had been going a little over the speed limit, so when I was pulled over I cursed myself, not only because I knew I would get fined, but also it was difficult to speak to the Guardia. The man who spoke to me drew a picture of a speed camera and said I was doing 107 in an 80 zone. They had a photo of me he said. Then came the unusual bit, he said I had to pay him €70 in cash. Luckily I had it on me, and he did give me a receipt, but I still to this day do not know if that is the legitimate way of dealing with speeding fines. At least we now had transport for a couple of weeks. We could have a nice time during Mark's visit, and hopefully the car would get sorted.

Over the next few weeks, we had to make regular pilgrimages down to Malaga to renew the hire on the car. Each time we went into Montoro, we drove past where the car had been left, and it still had not been moved. We would speak to Keith and he said that his friend in the garage was going to pick it up that week, so we just kept waiting. This was our first real experience of the mañana effect. While mañana means literally morning or tomorrow, if a workman or an office worker tells you something will happen 'mañana' it generally means it will happen, but not today. Maybe tomorrow, maybe the day after. Maybe! We were beginning to get frustrated, and of course the situation was costing us money to keep hiring cars. We still hadn't sold the house, and we were getting by but trying to save the pennies as best we could.

Our days comprised basic, menial tasks. The ladies would do the hand-washing and Chris and I would go out in hunter/gatherer mode and collect and chop the firewood for that night. At the time we didn't have a chainsaw so we were using two old handsaws that had been left behind, and it would take us at least two hours a day to prepare the evening's wood. I think the car situation and the lack of money had a detrimental effect on Frankie and Chris's attitude to our new lives. It was a difficult time for us all, so they decided to have a few days back in Brighton to see their friends and to make a few decisions. At the time I remember saying to Lorna that I wasn't sure if they would come back at all!

They did, however, return and we collected them from the airport, but they both seemed pretty quiet. We decided to stop for a meal, at a restaurant, to break up the journey.

"Is everything all right Frankie, you both seem very quiet," Lorna asked.

"To be honest Mum, I don't really think it's working for us living here. We haven't got any money and we can't even go out on our own." We had hoped to be able to buy a little run-around car that Chris and Frankie could use, but not having sold the house, our hands were tied. "We just thought it would be a bit different to this. We had a really good time when we were home, we miss our friends and I think it would be better if we went back."

Chris joined in, "We can live at my Mum's for a while, and we will both get jobs and we'll be able to save up for our own place, and of course we'll visit loads."

Lorna was devastated but we sympathised. We both understood their decision and as Lorna has said many times since, I'm not sure how many 19-year-olds would have been able to stick it out in the wilderness.

They planned to go back at the end of April, which

meant they were here to help us with preparing for the alpaca arrivals, which was now due to happen in the next couple of weeks, at the start of April. We were grateful for the help and of course it meant Lorna and Frankie were able to have some quality time before they returned. Although it was a difficult time, particularly for Lorna, it was a bit like a weight had been lifted: there had been an escalating level of tension in the air as it became obvious that it wasn't really working for the youngsters.

Chapter 14
Problems with my Waterworks

Animal count: One dog, one feral cat, two feral kittens (The mother cat that was living around the olive mill gave birth to two little kittens, but they were all so wild, we seldom saw them) and one pot-bellied pig.

"Alan!" Frankie hollered. "Erm, the never-ending water pipe has stopped." This was the name we had given to the pipe that came into our house and filled our *'deposito'*, and we had been told it never stopped. I know now that the water originates from a spring, deep in the hillside, but at the time I was blissfully unaware and just accepted that water ran freely to the house.

"Okay," I said, worried. "Chris, we have got a job to do!" I shouted, for a bit of moral support.

Chris and I went out to investigate, not really knowing what to look for or where to look, but we noticed Miguel out and about on his tractor, so we called out to him, and shouted in our ridiculously bad Spanish *"Problema, con agua"*.

He trundled over and had a look at a part of our supply pipe that comes out of the ground and has a tap attached to it. He opened the tap and some dirty water gushed out, but then it stopped. He said lots of things, but the only word we understood was *"limpia"* which means clean. We didn't really understand what he meant and he obviously realised this, so he took us up the hill to where our spring comes out of the hill. What it looks like is a little stone cupboard in the hillside with a metal door.

Obviously, I have concluded over time, someone found the source of the spring and, using drystone walling techniques, built a stone well that the water filters through and drips into, with a draining hole at the bottom from which a pipe runs all the way down the hill and back up to our house. From what we could make out, Miguel was explaining that this hole had become blocked, hence the dirty water, and therefore the lack of water now. What we needed to do was clean out the well hole. Miguel demonstrated this by removing his shirt to reveal a remarkably hairy chest and delving into the well, emerging with a handful of filthy smelly mud, and gesturing that this needed removing. What we had to do, was drain the well by undoing the pipe from the outside and letting the water run away, allowing us to clean the bottom of the well.

There is a drop of about three feet when the water is emptied from the well, so I had to lean into the water. The mud collected at the bottom was thoroughly unpleasant-smelling and wet, and therefore heavy. Of course, at the same time as leaning in and cleaning the well, the water was still dripping from above, so one ended up covered in water and mud and smelling foul and unpleasant too.

Once we had managed to clean out the well, it started to fill up again, and we waited for our water to start flowing. But it didn't. So we again had to call Miguel to come and explain the ancient Spanish plumbing system to us. This time we had to work our way down the pipe to every connection and let the air out, as air blocks won't allow the water to flow. With wet hands, we worked our way through half a dozen of these connections, and although by the end we were both suffering with blisters from undoing and retightening the pipes, we managed to start the water flowing.

This was my first lesson in Spanish farming DIY and plumbing, but I have become much more adept over the years and I can very often work out a way around a problem if I need to.

That hurdle cleared, we were ready for the next big one. The alpacas were going to be delivered and we were officially going to be alpaca breeders!

Chapter 15
Alpaca Arrival

"How are we going to cope in summer?" I asked Lorna.

"I don't know. I mean I know we were told it would be hot, but damn, this is hot!" Lorna laughed.

It was a bit of a shock to the system. By moving in January, we had thought we would be able to acclimatise during the year and by summer we would hopefully be able to cope, but this was intense and worrying. Over the years we have lived here we have learnt that very rarely does it get hot gradually, but normally there is a day, probably in June, when the atmosphere just feels different, hotter. We wake up feeling hot and just look at each other and know summer has arrived. The only thing was, it was April. This was an unseasonal heatwave, and the wind was blowing up from the Sahara desert in Africa, bringing with it the blazing hot air, and of course the red dust. This wind is known as the *'Sirocco'*.

"Do you know what?" I said sitting at the table drenched in sweat, "My eyelids are sweating!"

Lorna laughed at me, but it was true. I had never in my life been aware of my eyelids sweating before. That is how hot it was.

"And Peter is bringing the alpacas tomorrow - that will be fun in this weather!" I exclaimed.

Peter arrived early the following morning, having set off before sunrise to avoid the heat, to make the journey as comfortable as possible for the alpacas. We greeted Peter with hugs and hearty handshakes and there was a noticeable nervous excitement in the air.

We had prepared a paddock for the girls, Black Dancer and Cassandra, to use while we prepared the rest of the land around the house. We had erected simple, but pretty, two bar fencing around the area and Frankie had spent weeks painstakingly gathering stones and rocks, and building miniature dry stone walls around the bottom of the fencing. A key point in our research highlighted the fact that alpacas do not challenge fencing; that is to say, they will stay where you put them, not go through, over or under the fence. It all looked lovely.

Peter reversed the trailer up to the gate and I lowered the tailgate.

"Okay!" I shouted.

Peter exited the car. "This is it, are you sure you're ready to be alpaca breeders?"

We all replied in unison, "Yes!"

He ushered the girls down the ramp and into their new home. We waited for a few minutes, and Peter, on a bit of a schedule said, "Do you want me to catch them, so you can hold them before I go?"

Frankie's eyes lit up, "Yes, please."

It would be good for us to see the expert at work, for future reference.

Peter's approach to getting hold of an alpaca, is the unsubtle version. Corner and grab the animal, then hold on tight, a technique that has landed him on his backside on more than one occasion.

"Your side forward, this side back," Peter was directing, as we neared the fence "Okay, okay, slowly now."

As Peter made his clumsy lunge forward, Cassandra calmly turned and jumped right through the middle of the fencing. Not wanting to be separated from Cassandra, Black Dancer followed suit.

"So much for not challenging fencing," I joked.

"Um, well, maybe they are a bit stressed from the journey, but you're going to have to fix that fencing!" We looked at each other trying to suppress a giggle, it was like being told off by a teacher. "Anyway, I need to be off, I'm sure you'll manage. And don't forget, fix that fencing!"

He was climbing into his car with a wry smile on his face. He left us with a toot and a wave, and there we were waving our arms and gesturing at these bloody animals to get back in their paddock.

"Left a bit, right a bit, that's it, slowly, slowly, don't let her through, uuurrrrgggggghhhh," as once again they evaded us.

Eventually Frankie said, "I'll get some food!"

Well of course, as Frankie brought the food in, the girls jumped calmly through the fence immediately and began munching away.

"Maybe we should have fed them first!" she said with a smile. "C'mon Chris, we've got our orders, we've got fencing to fix."

We hunted through the barns and stables to find any old planks and fence posts we could use to keep the girls in. Our lovely two-bar fencing was long gone as it became hastily bodged-together three-bar fencing. We even had to remove Frankie's handiwork as the walls had started to fall down already and we didn't want any animal injuries. That was that, we were now alpaca breeders, at the forefront of the exciting new Spanish alpaca industry, and ready for riches to start flowing our way (We are still waiting now, four years later).

For the first weeks of our alpaca ownership, we became somewhat local celebrities, and were summoned out of the house, usually by cars tooting or people shouting to us. We spoke to all manner of local famers and officials, who had heard about the 'Ingles' and the *'animales locos'*.

We had to endure all the normal questions that you would expect in England, 'Why do you have alpacas?' 'Can you eat them?' and 'Can you milk them?' however, of course, all in Spanish. We managed to refine the answers over time, and can now talk quite comfortably about alpacas; ask us about cars, however, or gardening and we struggle. We gradually began to realise that many of the Spanish are very different to us in our attitudes with regard to animals, as well as the multitude of stray dogs you have to get used to here.

The Spanish just don't understand why you would

keep and breed an animal that doesn't produce meat for your family or milk either. A goat produces both of these and costs a fraction of the price. The only animals the Spanish seem to keep, that fits this description, are their horses. As far as we can tell, horses are a kind of status symbol: the more you have, the more important or wealthy you are, however it does not necessarily mean you care for those animals any better.

One day there was a commotion outside and a tooting of a car horn, so I looked out of the window only to find a car of the *'Guardia Civil'* and three uniform-clad policemen, complete with guns. With all the horror stories you hear about expat's homes being demolished or being fined for doing things wrong, I live in fear of something like this happening to us. Thankfully, one of the policemen only wanted to put his new camera phone to good use and have his picture taken with the alpacas, and after speaking with us for a few minutes the alpacas had worked their magic and they were all smiles. An alpaca cannot fail to brighten your day!

A few days later when we were feeding the girls one evening, an older man pulled up outside, with a young girl of about 10. The man was Ramon, in his mid-60s, only just about five-foot-tall, tanned leathery skin, with slick, black, brylcreemed hair like a 1950's film star. He wore brown trousers at least one size too big for him, held up by a belt fashioned from the string that holds bales of hay together and a smart shirt buttoned up to the top, even in the blazing heat.

He made a beeline for Lorna, and was all sweetness and light, and doe eyes. He boasted about his black hair, unlike Miguel, who he was saying is grey, and I imagine much less virile. Ramon is like an ageing lothario, with a twinkle in his eye, and a gap-toothed smile. Whenever he approaches for a little chat, he always heads straight for Lorna, unless it involves business, then it just wouldn't do to discuss it with a woman!

Juani, his daughter, was excited by the alpacas, and was learning English at school, but the lessons so far seemed to have reached 'Hello', 'Yes' and 'No'. She was, however, very proud of herself. It transpired that Ramon owned a large amount of land near us, with thousands of olive trees, and he got his wallet out of his trouser pocket and took out a €50 note, gesturing that it was for one of the girls. We thanked him, but said a gracious no, we needed them for breeding!

Chapter 16
Two Young, Too Rural

Animal count: One dog, one feral cat, two feral kittens, one pot-bellied pig, two alpacas (Cassandra and Black Dancer)

All too soon we had reached the day before Frankie and Chris were due to leave. For the previous week the atmosphere had become increasingly tense, as both mum and daughter began to dread saying goodbye. Even though by this time we all agreed that the right decision had been made, Frankie was 19, and this was a pivotal moment in her life, probably even more so than just moving out of home in the UK. She was flying off to start her own life and make her way in the world. For that last week Chris and I did our best to keep our heads down.

In the evening, we decided to visit a local bar in town that we had heard was used by the few English families who live here, and the owner even speaks a little English too. When we pulled up outside the bar, and parked the car, there was a group of Spanish teenagers outside who proceeded to stare directly at us, obviously noticing our Englishness (Chris's Arsenal football shirt probably didn't help). Being teenagers themselves, this raised the heckles of both Frankie and Chris, and under her breath I could hear Frankie saying, "What are you looking at!"

In England, staring at each other is considered a challenge, especially to teenagers, but here it is just part of their nature. The Spanish stare at everybody, even their countrymen, particularly the older people who like nothing more than standing and watching a workman at the roadside. The old Spanish men can wile away many an hour watching somebody working, either on a building site or working on the roads, sometimes chatting to them and no doubt putting the world to rights. Sometimes, just watching in silence!

Once inside the bar we were greeted by Antonio and his latest female companion. This time the girl was young, very young in fact, and rather vocal, no doubt encouraged by more than a couple of alcoholic beverages, and she was hanging from Antonio's neck. He tilted his head to one side and raised his eyebrows to me as if to say, "What can I do?" The girl was introduced to us as Petra, and although she spoke a little English, she seemed to be Russian or Eastern European.

Petra seemed to be quite fun, so when Antonio visited the bathroom, we were talking about him and I jokingly said, "You know he's 55 don't you?"

Petra's eyes widened, "Fack off, iz 'ee?" and "Facking 45 'ee tell me," as profanities spewed from her mouth like a 20-stone trucker. I was hysterical; I felt as though it was just a little payback for his previous behaviour. She stormed off towards the gents' toilet and literally dragged him out, demanding that he show her his passport and prove he was only 45. It was hilarious for us, but Antonio was very unhappy and left immediately. At least it had gone some way to lighten the mood for the evening and we were able to enjoy a pleasant meal together before heading home at about 10 o'clock to finish off the packing and have a reasonably early night, before setting off for the airport the following morning.

On our return to the Olive Mill, outside our gate were the two most stunning, most enormous Spanish mastiff dogs, lying across the road. One had a long coat and was white in colour, almost like a large retriever, and the other had short, black hair. Both were beautiful dogs and they sat proudly outside our fence, until Chris got out of the car to open the gate. The dogs approached him and were extremely friendly. They were all over him, jumping up on him, and one even had his paws on his shoulders, licking him and being affectionate. We drove in through the gate and managed, somehow, to keep the dogs out, thinking that, as they were so beautiful, they must belong to somebody, and surely they would make their own way home.

After two hours, they were still there when I went to lock the gate for the night. Maybe, I hoped, they would be gone by morning.

We had to leave just after six o'clock the following morning, and as we left the house it was freezing cold: there was ice on the car and the alpacas' water had frozen over. Outside, these two dogs were still sitting in the road, oblivious to the cold. Once again they were friendly and wanted our attention as we loaded the car. Maybe they were trying to tell Frankie and Chris to stay?

As we drove off, they reassumed their position on the road, and I said to Lorna, "If they are still there tonight, when we get home, we must try and find the owner, surely they must live somewhere around here."

It gave us a slight distraction from the inevitable tension of the morning, and as we made the three-hour journey down the motorway with hardly a word spoken, the only sounds being occasional, involuntary sniffles coming from the direction of Frankie or Lorna.

At the airport we queued up for check-in, and decided that as there were visits booked both to the UK for Lorna, and for the kids back to us in the summer, we should say a quick goodbye at the front of the queue and not draw it out too long.

As we reached our turn in the queue, the lady behind the counter weighed the bags.

"I'm afraid these bags are overweight, both are over 35kg and the limit is only 23kg," said the girl apologetically. "There is going to be a charge of €150 before we can let you on, I'm afraid."

Frankie burst in to tears, and this tipped Lorna over the edge and they fell into each other's arms sobbing.

It was hard for Chris and I to watch, so I said, "Okay, don't worry, I'll go and sort this out, you two wait here. Come on Chris, come with me."

A few minutes later we returned, and it was time to say goodbye.

Lorna was in a state, Frankie was in a state, and Chris and I didn't know where to look. We all gave each other a hug and off they went. Lorna has always found goodbyes difficult, but that was probably the hardest one ever.

Thinking we should get going, get home and try and relax, I ushered Lorna towards the car park, but she stopped me in my tracks and told me to sit down on a nearby bench, where she told me that she had arranged for my Mum and brother to visit as a surprise for my birthday, which was the following day, but they weren't arriving until 9 pm that night, so we had to wait a full 12 hours. We managed to dwindle away the day and collected my family that evening. By then we were exhausted, physically and mentally, and we still had a three-hour drive back up the motorway.

As we approached the house Lorna said, "What are we going to do if the dogs are still here? How will we find the owners?"

"Hmm, I don't know, I had forgotten about them to be honest, let's just see if they are there first."

When we arrived back, at just about midnight, there was no sign of the dogs. It was like a metaphor, Frankie and Chris had gone and so had the dogs. To this day we have never seen those two beautiful dogs around here, we don't know where they came from or where they went, but, they had gone!

There was something that we had never considered before we moved. Would we be able to cope with, not only the isolation of living in such a rural location, but also each other, 24 hours a day, seven days a week? Over the next few months we had numerous occasions where Lorna would be in tears, and I would not know what to say or do. She was desperately missing her children, plus, to put it very simply, she was missing talking to people. Her job as a dance teacher was very social and meant lots of interaction both with parents and children.

On more than one occasion I asked, "Do you want to go home?"

"No, no," Lorna always insisted, but each little thing

74

that happened to us ground away at our dream that little bit more.

Chapter 17
Carlos

"Okay, I'm going into town to get some medicine for you. Just stay in bed and don't get up, I won't be long," Lorna said as she walked out of the door.

I was ill in the bed, with a touch of man-flu, and feeling pretty bad. On her return I heard the gate open, followed shortly after by the front door.

Lorna had a sad look on her face. "I got your medicine, but when I went out, Miguel was there, and he said there was a dog, looking a bit thin and hiding in the bush. I saw him, but he was very nervous, so I left him there and went to town. But he is still there now, and I don't know what to do. Up until now, we have been so good about not taking in every stray we've seen, but I don't think I can leave him outside." She was rambling a bit, and I could tell she wanted to go out and see the dog.

"Why don't you take him some water and a little food. Once he has got his strength back, maybe he will go home?" I said.

"Okay, I'll try that."

After about ten minutes, Lorna returned.

"He wolfed down that food, the poor thing is starving. He's really thin too, and I think he's injured. He keeps holding his paw in the air. When I walked towards him outside, I could hear this thumping, and I couldn't work it out, but it was his tail bashing the ground."

"Is he still outside in the bush?"

"No, he followed me in. He's lying down in the courtyard outside, he won't go back out. Why don't you come and see him?"

So I dragged myself from my sick bed, and went out to see the dog. I was greeted by a very nervous, ginger and white, bony little thing. And sure enough he was holding his paw up and, to be honest, he looked in a bad way.

"Oh dear, look at him," I said sadly. I looked at the paw. "There doesn't seem to be much wrong with his paw though, but look, he's got a tight chain around his neck. Let's get that off."

I had to use pliers to free the chain. Although we had been strong to date, I knew immediately we were going to keep this dog. The fatal mistake is feeding them. Once you do that, they look at you like you are their world and it is very hard to send them away again.

"But, he's a stray so he can sleep outside. He will be fine, he's used to it." I said.

"Okay," Lorna smiled ruefully.

The next day we had some exciting news as Penny phoned to say that Bermuda, our white girl, had given birth to a healthy baby boy. We made the drive down to Ronda to see this new arrival. When we saw the cria, he was all legs, so we decided to name him Basil, after Basil Fawlty. It was a really lovely day for us holding that new baby and Bermuda, the girl with the fearsome reputation, was an amazing mother. We were starting to have a lovely time. This, however, was all about to change.

I have found somewhere to live! After a few days of trawling the countryside, since running away from those men with the guns, finally someone has taken pity on me. Today, a lovely lady found me outside her house. There was a man too, but he was on a big machine and it made me nervous.

The lady brought me out some water, and a little food, so I followed her in. She seemed kind, so I wasn't scared. There is another dog at the house, but she seems to be quite old, and a little bit grumpy, but she didn't try to hurt me. After a while, a man came out, and he took off the chain around my neck, which was good because it was starting to hurt me. The man cleaned me with some water, and then gave me some more food. My sad look seems to be working. I tried to follow them into their house, but the man made me stay outside, but at least there I feel safe, and I managed to have a good sleep. I hope they let me stay here.

Carlos

Chapter 18
Black Dancer

Animal count : Two dogs (Geri and Carlos), one feral cat, two feral kittens, one pot-bellied pig and two alpacas.

During May a team of shearers came over to Spain, organised by Peter, and visited the farms of the alpaca owners in Andalucía. The team was from Australia, and spent the summer shearing, travelling throughout Europe.

To our horror and surprise, when they turned over Black Dancer she was suffering from a terrible skin condition all over her stomach and the tops of her legs. We felt terrible that we hadn't noticed, but it wasn't something we had been told to check and how often do you look under an animal? We were advised to get some special skin treatment from the UK, which of course we ordered immediately.

A week or so after the shearing, we were feeding the alpacas one evening when Black Dancer began to cough and splutter. Sometimes this happens, if they eat too fast or have too big a mouthful, but normally it clears itself after a couple of minutes.

This was different; it didn't clear, and she started to cough up her green rumen everywhere. We called Manuel the vet, and I went and collected him. This was going to be his first alpaca experience and it was getting dark too. By the time we got back to the house it was completely black, so we had to drive our small hire car into the alpaca paddock so that we could use the headlights for Manuel to see to work on Black Dancer.

Manuel tried to manipulate her throat to try and clear any obstruction, but when this failed he tried to use a long tube to insert in her throat in the hope this would clear it. Eventually this seemed to work, but Manuel was concerned. We told him about the skin condition and he felt that she was a very unwell animal, and we should call him in the morning.

After a terrible night's sleep for us, Black Dancer seemed a little brighter. We spoke to Manuel and he said he was still very wary and would give us some products to use on her skin to help her in the meantime. He wanted her to be as comfortable as possible, but he was still concerned that she was a very sick animal. Two days passed and she started to eat a little more and we felt she was improving slightly, slowly but slightly.

One morning I got up and looked out of the window and shouted, "Oh shit!"

Lorna said, "What?"

"Something on the ground, a baby or something, but it might be dead."

My stomach had dropped and nerves and adrenalin were shooting through me. There was something on the ground covered in blood. We had heard about a few possible birthing problems, and I was due to be going to England the following day for a course on alpaca birthing. I grabbed some scissors and a clean towel and ran down to the paddock.

When I got there it didn't look good. I found a small baby, still in the birthing sac, not moving. I split the bag but the tiny baby inside was dead. It was our first experience of an alpaca birth and it was not a good one.

Our research had shown that alpacas generally have very easy births, and do not need much in the way of intervention; however this one was not to be. A couple of years down the line I can look back and know that Black Dancer aborted that baby, probably due to being very sick herself. Animals and nature have a way of dealing with problems and she couldn't have coped if the baby had survived. Her body was giving her the best chance of getting better.

We spoke to a number of different people and the general consensus was that we should get an autopsy on the foetus. This meant keeping it overnight, to our horror, in a freezer bag, sealed in our fridge. The following morning, Lorna would have the horrendous job of taking me to the train station, and then taking the baby to Manuel to organise the autopsy. I felt terrible leaving Lorna to cope with all this but we had paid for the course, and now more than ever, we felt that we needed the knowledge. I was sure Lorna could cope.

We left early the following morning. Although it was dark, Black Dancer did not look in great shape. Lorna said she would collect Manuel on her way back from the station. A few hours later I reached Gatwick, turned on the phone, and immediately called Lorna.

"How's things?" I asked.

"Not great," she replied. "To be honest I'm not sure she is going to survive. It took me hours to sort out the baby's autopsy: I had to carry him around Montoro in that bloody Lidl bag for hours. By the time I got home with Manuel, Black Dancer didn't look good."

I was distraught to think that Lorna was having to deal with this on her own. I was completely out of my comfort zone, and powerless to help.

I managed to telephone Penny and explain what was going on, and to his eternal credit, Peter dropped everything and drove the three hours to Montoro to help and support Lorna until I could return. In actual fact, Peter had arrived while Lorna was taking Manuel back to his surgery in town and, when she arrived home, Peter had scaled the fence and was inside attending to Black Dancer. I will never be able to thank him enough for that.

For my part, when I reached my Mum's house in the UK, I fell into her arms and cried like a baby. I hadn't cried for years, and God only knows what my Mum thought, but I just didn't know what to do. Once I had got my head together I managed to change my return flight and went straight back the following morning. Lorna collected me from the station and told me how amazing both Peter and Manuel had been. We had a routine of injections and treatments for Black Dancer. Lorna had it all written down.

Before now we hadn't really comprehended that we would need to learn how to administer injections to animals. It is not as easy as you think, there are different ways to give different drugs and you have to be strong, plus you have to consider carefully where that thermometer needs to go when taking a temperature! We were thrust into this by events that were unfolding around us. Although I knew the situation was bad, I felt a bit better at least knowing I was there to help, and we would get through it together.

After two days of hourly treatments, through the day and night - and very little sleep - on the third morning I woke up early and went out to check on the girls, only to find that Black Dancer had died that morning. It was very distressing, but we truly could not have done any more than we did; we gave her every chance.

"I'll go out and move Black Dancer, maybe try to get her into the car," I said to Lorna.

"I don't think I can lift her body Alan, it's too heavy for me, and I just don't think I can do it."

"Okay, I'll see what I can do on my own."

I spoke to both Peter and Manuel, and Peter suggested that we could arrange for Cassandra to move back to their farm for a few months, until she had her baby, and give us a chance to get our heads together again. Alpacas are herd animals, and we had heard stories of animals dying of loneliness without companions, so this was a good option. Manuel gave up his whole Sunday to help me move the body and transport it to the University where they carried out an autopsy and disposed of the body for us.

I was worried about Cassandra being on her own overnight, so I said to Lorna, "I'm going to go out and sit with her, to make sure she is alright."

I went out during the wildest electrical storm I have ever seen, planning to sit with her through the night to make sure she didn't die of loneliness. The sky was an angry purple colour, and there was fork lightening all along the horizon, but no thunder. It was unnervingly quiet. Cassandra settled down and to be honest seemed more uneasy with me there, than on her own, so after an hour or two I decided she would be okay, and went in to try and sleep.

The following day Lorna and I breathed a sigh of relief, although we felt incredibly sad, as Cassandra was collected. We had never thought that it would be like this. When we spoke to people after and since, we are always told, "If you keep livestock, you have to deal with dead stock too!" It is true, and maybe obvious, but no one tells you that when you are buying the animals. No one says to you, "How are you going to cope when they get sick or die?" Maybe they should!

Chapter 19
Bingo

Animal count : Two dogs, one feral cat, two feral kittens and one pot-bellied pig.

After a couple of weeks of self-imposed exile, we were starting to feel a little more like facing the world. It just so happened that, on that day, Miguel was out and about once again. He called out to me, and was chatting away, asking about the alpacas, where they were, etc, and I did my best to explain the problems we had had. I told him that Cassandra was okay, but had gone to Ronda for a while. He looked at me sympathetically, and then almost as though a light bulb had gone off in his head, an idea occurred to him.

"*¡Esta noche, ocho en punto, AQUI!*" This translated as, 'Tonight, eight o'clock, HERE!' He also threw in Adamuz (a very small local village) and "*¡Mucha cerveza!*"

"Erm, Lorna, I think I might have got us into something," I started quietly. "Miguel was outside, and he invited us out tonight. Well, I say invited - he told me he is picking us up at eight o'clock."

"Where are we going?"

"Hmm, I don't really know that. He said Adamuz, and he said lots of beer, of course."

"Well, maybe it will do us good to get out for a bit, I could do with a laugh!" Lorna likes any opportunity to mix with the locals, and embarrass ourselves with our truly inept Spanish.

At eight o'clock, we waited outside for Miguel to arrive, dressed up in our 'going out clothes'. We had no idea where we going but at least we had made some effort, and better to be safe than sorry.

When Miguel arrived we clambered onto the back of his battered, old, pick-up truck, either side of his daughter Andrea, who was holding a rather large box of assorted and oddly shaped vegetables. Miguel raised his hands in the air, and said loudly "Vin-ho!" as if this explained the box. Off we went, with a little look of trepidation to each other.

After about five kilometres on our road, we made a turn signposted for Adamuz and followed a winding road for about 10 minutes, before pulling into a crowded car park, in the middle of nowhere, outside what seemed to be the equivalent of a roadside bar. Outside there was a collection of small animal pens, some with chickens and turkeys in, a couple with goats in, and there was even an old donkey tied to a post outside the bar. We walked into the bar a few steps behind Miguel and Olga, feeling incredibly conspicuous as the Spanish farmers present turned to look in our direction.

Inside it was like a farmers' convention: the bar was heaving, ninety percent full of men in blue overalls direct from working in the country. The few women that there were there could have been related to Olga, all of them were rather round and dumpy. In Spain, or certainly Montoro, the women all seem to be incredibly slim and beautiful and then, at a particular age, the olive oil seems to begin to settle on their hips. The air in the bar was thick with smoke and it was difficult to see from one end to the other. There was a loud hum of chatter from all around. "Luuuuuuuunnnnnaaaaaaaaa," we heard from near the bar. (None of our neighbours have ever got the hang of pronouncing Lorna's name correctly.) We spotted Ramon at the bar and went over. There was much handshaking, backslapping and cheek-kissing but the conversation passed us by, although we did again pick up this word "¡Vin-ho!"

Ramon bought us a drink, and once again I had to endure the inevitable laughter at my expense about my refusal to drink alcohol. "Solo Coco-Cola" and much hilarity followed. I was then offered a cigarette. I had to bite the bullet and say, *"No gracias, no fumar,"* The laughter grew, and Ramon said, "You do sex?" Oh dear, I was certainly going to be the figure of fun that night!

After about 30 minutes, a rather large man entered at the front of the room. He had a cigar protruding from his mouth, a rather large stomach hanging over his trousers and a grey handlebar moustache on his round face. He arranged an upturned crate for himself to be seated on and a small table, onto which he placed a large, old fashioned tombola. A queue started to form at the man's desk, everybody either waiting in line with a box of vegetables similar to Miguel's or with a little white ticket. Once the offerings were handed over, they were given a bundle of photocopied papers.

As Miguel returned to the table we clicked as to what was going on. The photocopies were of old bingo cards, and Miguel had got us some too. We smiled at each other; our big night out was farmers' bingo. All these, hard-drinking, tough-as-nails farmers were all sitting down to play a friendly game of bingo. This, however, proved to be bingo with a difference.

The first winner won a selection of seedlings for the allotment. The second winner won Miguel's box of irregular home-grown vegetables. As we worked our way through the games, the crowd got rowdier and noisier as more and more alcohol was consumed. The atmosphere was approaching fever-pitched. Nearing the final three games, to our surprise two of the animal containers were brought in. The first had about four chickens in it and the second had two young turkeys. Finally, a proud-looking young man entered with two goats on leads and tied them to a post by the stage. These animals were the last three prizes of the night.

To be honest, as much as we would have loved one of the little goats, we were never going to win any prizes, as the man calling the bingo numbers was speaking so fast we could barely understand. If we got fifty per cent of the numbers right I would be surprised. Our only fear was that the animals would be slaughtered for the winners but thankfully they were all taken back to their country houses - although I am sure they have all ended up on many a dinner plate since.

At one point in the evening Lorna plucked up the courage for a trip to the bar for us. There was a small area where the women sat knitting, with children or grandchildren around them, with a bullfight being shown on a small television in the corner. It was one of these ladies who put down her knitting and served the drinks, rather perturbed to have to stop what she was doing, and of course interrupt watching her bullfight!

As we left the bar, feeling slightly bewildered by the events of the evening, the large man who was doing the calling was climbing onto the donkey to go home. We laughed to see this big guy clambering on to his 'steed' and then steadying himself for his journey. I wonder if you can be fined for being drunk in charge of a donkey?

Suddenly, Ramon came running over to us, carrying two scraggy looking chickens upside down by the legs. He thrust them into our hands, and laughed as we must have looked confused. We tried to refuse but he just gestured us away, so we had to sit in the back of the car each with a scraggy brown chicken on our lap. Every so often, we would hit a bump in the road and the chicken would jump about. My chicken pecked my hand one time and I let it go: all hell broke loose in the car. The chicken was jumping around bashing the windows, and we were laughing and screaming. Miguel had to pull the car to the side of the road, and grabbed the chicken forcibly and pushed it to me with a look of, don't let it go again!

Miguel took us home, and every few minutes in the back of the car we just looked at each other and smiled; we couldn't believe the evening we had just had. It was probably the first time we had laughed properly since the death of Black Dancer and it had been just what we had needed. We thanked Miguel and Olga for the evening and left the car with our chickens.

As it was dark, we were able to use Geri's large pet carrier for them to sleep in for the night, and we could move them in the morning. We were left in complete darkness with only the brightness of the stars in the sky. I swear, there are a million more stars here than there ever were back in Brighton or maybe we just take a bit more time to appreciate them here.

"We're going to be okay, you know," I said to Lorna.

"I know we will."

We felt as though we had turned a little corner, and collapsed into bed, exhausted!

Chapter 20
First Cordoban Summer

Animal count: Two dogs, three feral cats, one pot-bellied pig and two chickens. (Due to a large amount of bum wiggling, we decided to name the new chickens Beyonce and J-lo.)

Our first Andalucían summer stretched on throughout four months of blazing weather and long, hot summer evenings. When we had originally visited the Olive Mill it had been August and it had been hot, but you simply cannot ever be prepared enough for living through months and months of extreme temperatures. In the UK people will do anything possible to avoid being seen sweating, but here you have to accept it as part of life - from waking up some mornings with sweat-drenched hair, to leaving your car with sweat-drenched clothes. In fact, any physical activity whatsoever results in a sweat. Even sleeping in close proximity to another human being becomes impossible. It is necessary to find yourself a position, laid out on the bed in such a way that parts of your own body do not touch another part of your own body, let alone someone else's! Eventually this results in a kind of demented starfish approach to sleeping.

We survive the summer by siesta-ing during the afternoon, having a series of cool or cold baths and showers, and much like the natives, getting work done early in the morning, or late in the evening. We like to visit the local park late at night when, after sunset at about 10 pm all the families come out and socialise: the children play, maybe have a drink and something to eat. It's lovely to see such a family atmosphere flourishing in this day and age, and we can wile away the hours until two or three in the morning just watching the world go by.

One major, major high point of the summer for us was accepting an offer on our house in the UK. Nearly one year after initially putting it up for sale, and after numerous reductions and negotiations, we did finally accept an offer. We did though, end up losing around £70,000 on our original price and, by this time, the crisis was driving down the exchange rate, so we found ourselves much less financially secure than we thought we would be. However, at last we were able to start decorating and renovating some parts of the Olive Mill.

One common mistake, made by many an expat, not just us, is to use only people they know, or who speak the same language. We fell into this trap when we wanted work doing on the Olive Mill. There was lots of decorating that needed doing and we felt we were up to managing that for ourselves, but we approached Neil, the previous owner, about giving us a price for repairing the roof on an empty shell area, and then creating a large open-plan living space, with tiled floors, electrics and all the plumbing. We were happy with his ideas and the price he quoted, and not knowing anyone else, we made a deal with Neil to start as soon as the house sale in the UK was completed.

While we had been talking to Neil, we got onto the subject of our car and its ongoing off the road state. We said that the people in Montoro were not being very helpful, and that it had been sitting on the roadside for months. We had paid a tow truck to take it to Cordoba, where we could get the Mitsubishi garage to look at it, and hopefully give us a price to fix it. After a week, and over €500 for a diagnosis they had quoted us over €7,000 Euros to fix the car, so it had been sitting outside their garage ever since and we didn't really know what to do next.

Neil told us about 'Jack, the German', a mechanic on the coast, who might be able to help us if he could locate a second-hand engine. If so, he could do the work and have it back on the road for around €1,800. Well, obviously this was music to our ears, and although still a lot of money, we needed to do something. We were still spending out on hire cars, and the car had cost us €4,500 so we really needed it back on the road.

So one day we met Jack the German in Cordoba. He was quite a scary, unsmiling man who chain-smoked and spoke only a few English words. He was wearing dark grey overalls, had grey hair and thick-rimmed glasses. We sent the car off with him and crossed our fingers: it had to be our best shot at getting it running again.

A few weeks later we went to collect the car, and even then he charged us an extra €200 over what we were expecting. We were beginning to feel like all the people we met were only out to get as much money as possible from us, only taking time to help us if there was something in it for them. It is a bit of a sad fact of the expat community that there are many tales of scams and cons, and they generally concentrate on the vulnerable and naïve. Even Alex, the man from whom we had bought the car and refused to help us, had scarpered back to the UK leaving behind a garage full of debt, and a wife and two kids stranded in Spain with no money.

Once we had collected our car, it didn't take long for us to realise that the air conditioning no longer worked. So, having collected the car in mid-August we now had to endure the hottest part of the summer in a vehicle without much-needed air conditioning. One journey we had to endure was a seven-hour round trip to collect the latest additions to our menagerie.

Ever since the two dogs that appeared on the day that Frankie and Chris left, I had made up my mind that I wanted to get a Spanish mastiff (the Spanish call them *Mastin Español*). They are such large and loyal beautiful dogs, with amazing temperaments, plus they are noisy and make great guard dogs. On a visit to a coastal market, we got talking to a lady who worked for one of the many dog rescue centres that exist there.

"Really? Are you looking for a mastin? I might be able to help, let me make a call." She was on her mobile in a flash. Then she returned, smiling. "There is somebody we know, looking to re-home a brother and sister, who they rescued after they were abandoned with their ears chopped off and their tails wired. But they must be kept together!"

We looked at each other. The thought of these dogs having their tails wired and their ears chopped off was horrifying, but we hadn't wanted two; these dogs grow to be at least 60 kilos in size and two of these will eat their way through a lot of dog food.

We decided we would get in touch with the people and see what they said, but we knew we wouldn't be able to separate the brother and sister. We made contact with the current owner and told them about our house and land, and how we had been looking for one of these dogs, and then we had heard about their situation.

They were very keen for us to take both the dogs, as they had been thinking that they may be forced to have them put to sleep if they couldn't find homes for them. We discussed it over the next few days, talked about the pros and cons, but, in truth, I think we decided the minute we heard about them. We would take them.

We set out on the long journey to collect them, with the dog crate that we had brought Geri to Spain in. Thinking they were only 12-week-old puppies we could put them in there for the journey. We arrived at the house, three and a half hours later, very hot, and found two lolloping great lumps of puppy, with legs too long for their bodies and no control over them either. At 12 weeks old they weighed over 20 kilos each, and were already bigger than our other two dogs. No way were they going in the crate. We had to heave them into the back of the car, and hastily close the door so they couldn't escape.

The temperature gauge in the car as we set off read 45 degrees, and without the air conditioning, we planned to stop regularly for water and a break for the pups. We set off, bumping down the dusty track that led from the house to the road. Lorna was in the back seat and the dogs in the boot. After no more than 100 metres, we heard the most stomach-churning noise.

"Oh no, what on earth was that?" I asked.

"Err, Blue has just been sick," Lorna said, cringing.

We decided to press on hoping she would settle and feel a little better when we reached the smoother roads and the motorway. After about 30 minutes of heaving and retching, Blue seemed to calm down a little, only for Arthur, who had up until now, held his stomach together manfully, to start being travel sick.

"Whoah, and there goes Arthur!" Lorna exclaimed. "Oh dear this car is going to take some cleaning."

There was only one thing for it: we had to make only one stop on the journey and get home as quickly as possible. On our arrival we immediately grabbed a hose and as we opened the car, we grabbed the dogs before they could escape and hosed them down. This was followed by a major scrubbing and cleaning session in the back of the car. Ever since that day both the dogs will do anything to get out of travelling in the car, and even the vet has to come to our house to do their annual jabs. To make matters worse, Arthur is petrified of the vet and I have to do his injections myself.

Another major summer occurrence was the birth of our second alpaca cria, at Peter and Penny's farm. This time the mother was Cassandra, and she gave birth to a beautiful, white boy. We had been hoping for a coloured girl, but we were just glad it was healthy and breathing. We chose to name the baby Rafa, as Rafa Nadal had just won his first Wimbledon title. Also, Rafael means 'Healed by God'. His full name is Sunshine Rafael as Sunshine is the prefix for all the animals born on our farm.

Since Cassandra had returned to Peter's farm she had been isolated with one of our other girls, Lily. This was as a precaution, because we were unsure as to what Black Dancer had died of, and it was possible that Cassandra may have it too. We made a few lengthy trips to see Cassandra and little Rafa, and we were trying to prepare ourselves to have them back on our farm. Obviously with our previous experience, our anxiousness had been heightened.

Around this time, a few health issues arose on Peter's

farm, sadly resulting in some losses to their herd. Mostly, animals that had been imported from the UK, but it also affected some of those that were originally on their farm. There were some losses of babies and their mothers too. It was a horrible time, and we can only imagine what Peter and Penny had to go through. Sadly, our little Basil died during this period, but thankfully Bermuda, his mother, was okay. The problem meant that it became a blessing that Cassandra, Lily and Rafa had been isolated, as they would hopefully stay clear of any health issues the other animals may be harbouring.

Even without the animals being on our farm we were beginning to get paranoid, wondering what on earth we had got ourselves into, and dreading every phone call. Our thoughts and hearts were with Peter and Penny continually throughout this horrible time.

I don't know what on earth they are thinking now. First, they bring me this ginger boy, who is scared of his own shadow, and now they turn up with two huge dogs, one boy, one girl and yet, they only look like babies. They keep bashing me, and I try to tell them off but they just keep on. That's going to get annoying.

They seem to get more food than me, but at least the people make them sleep outside with the other one. They seem to know that I'm the boss, and they let me sleep in the house with them. The new boy though, he barks all night, it really is very disturbing. Maybe I will have to have a word with him.

Geri

Chapter 21
Christmas

Animal count: Four dogs (Geri, Carlos, Blue and Arthur), three feral cats, one pot-bellied pig and two chickens.

As we broke the back of our first summer in 'The Frying Pan', the days slowly started to shorten, and the heat gradually began to lessen. September was upon us and the house sale was completed. We were able to buy our first pots of paint, and finally able to start getting down to some work. I'm sure it is an image no one needs, but due to the heat, and to save on washing, we found it easiest and coolest to paint in our pants! It became much easier to just jump in the shower and wash paint off rather than try and remove it from clothes. So there we were, up ladders and painting walls, in the unflattering combination of pants, socks and trainers.

We were also able to set Neil to work, renovating our new open-plan living area, and repairing the ageing roof. This was where the bulk of our money was going, and we hoped we had made a good decision. We got on well with Neil: we had become friends and we felt we could trust him, and of course we spoke the same language. That meant Neil was around for a few months, so for four days a week we were not alone at the Mill. It made a nice change to have somebody around, but it did mean we had to start to paint and work in our clothes again. It also meant that at the weekends we also began to appreciate being on our own, enjoying the peace and tranquillity of our new home.

As we progressed into winter, the spectre of Lorna's first childless Christmas was beginning to loom on the horizon. We decided to try not to make too big a deal out of Christmas deciding to paint the new living area and keep ourselves busy. So we spent two weeks over Christmas, barring Christmas Day and Boxing day, outside in the cold painting. The skies were blue and clear, however the wind seemed to be coming from the north and it was bitterly cold - for those two weeks even our breath froze as we worked. We wore two layers of clothes and fingerless gloves.

On Christmas Day, we allowed ourselves a lie-in, and after Skyping with both of Lorna's kids, and of course a few tears, we decided to start a tradition for our new life. As the weather was sunny, we decided a barbecue would be a great idea, if only because we could!

We set up our outside dining area on our terrace and lit the barbecue. What we had not accounted for was that our new (animal) family would want to join in the celebrations. By now, Blue and Arthur had grown in to two very large, very playful puppies. They were six months old, and still growing of course: they were now up to our waists, and beginning to put on some bulk. In contrast to their size, they liked to play like Yorkshire terriers. After spending an hour cooking the food, standing guard over the barbecue just in case one of the dogs decided to make a launch at the grill, we sat down to eat. This is where things went slightly wrong.

Blue, who thinks she is the size of a chihuahua, tried to get under the table for a piece of meat she thought had been dropped. This alerted Arthur, who also tried to beat her to the tasty morsel, and we were unceremoniously pushed out of the way. The table wobbled, and wine and drinks spilled over the food. The next thing we knew, the table flipped and food, cutlery and drinks were spread about the terrace. An almighty melee ensued: dogs barking and fighting for scraps, us panicking over broken glass and china. Our Christmas dinner was turning into a worse fight than any dinner with the in-laws! We managed to restore order with the help of a cold hose and lots of water, but our new tradition was dead and buried before it had even begun. These days a cheap chicken from Lidl and some roast potatoes serves us just as well.

On Boxing Day, we went out to check out the Spanish sales. We drove to Cordoba, to a large shopping centre, and parked up. Busier than we expected, we entered the centre to find people with trolleys piled high and it was insanely busy. We wandered around for a while, then began to realise that there didn't seem to be any signs for sales. These people were still doing their Christmas shopping! We had been told about 'Day of the Kings' in Spain, 6th January, which was when the children traditionally received their presents, but we had thought that it was an extra celebration. In fact no, on Christmas Day the children may receive one present from Papa Noel, but their main celebration is on the 6th. It felt very alien to us, this concept.

Where we live, life is still very traditional, and although there are a few decorations hung up in both Montoro and Cordoba, the commercialism that we experience in the UK is not so evident here. Decorations and Christmas promotions don't start so early, and there is a much more laid back attitude to the celebrations. Here, the Christmas holiday is about spending time with families and not about how many presents you can buy your child. It's not until you step away from the way we have become in the UK that you realise how much we have lost as a society. It really is true what they say, in the UK we live to work, but here, truly they work to live!

Frankie managed to visit early in the New Year to take in the celebrations for King's Day. We decided we would go into Montoro to experience the arrival of the Kings. A parade to symbolise the arrival of the Kings at the birth of baby Jesus, this procession is put on in every town and village up and down Spain. This is the equivalent of our Christmas Eve. Children are very excited, as they will receive their presents the following day.

The parade was preceded by people old and young wandering up and down the street, gathering their empty bags and looking for the best spot to stand. We were unaware that as the procession makes its way through the streets, the people on the floats throw bundles and bundles of sweets, with great force. It's not unusual for children to be heard crying having being hit in the eye! There is an almighty scramble and all inhibitions go out of the window as children and adults alike crawl around on the ground collecting the hundreds of sweets. It was kind of hysterical to see all of the Spanish, particularly the well-dressed couples, joining in with the tradition. I'm not sure many people in the UK would lower themselves to join in, although I'm sure the kids would love it.

We made the best of the few days Frankie could manage to be here, and we had a second Christmas and even cooked a traditional dinner. We decided against a barbecue this time!

I really don't know what all the fuss was about. All we wanted to do was join in the party. The two other dogs, they were under the table sniffing around, why shouldn't we be allowed to go under there? And it's certainly not our fault if they drop their food on the floor, what do they think we are going to do, just let the others have it? No way. It smelt good, and I wanted my fair share. Okay, okay, so the old girl got a bit angry, anyway, all she does is moan, and the boy went away and hid. Well, we have tried to be friends with them, but when we try to play they just shout at us. At least my brother likes to play, so sometimes we run around and play fight. This new house seems to be a nice place, but those pesky cats, they drive me mad, and they make my brother really angry, and he barks at night, but hopefully soon we will be able to catch them and then they'll be sorry.

Blue

Chapter 22
The Alpacas Return

The day came in the middle of January, the day we had both been dreading, but also looking forward to. Almost a year to the day since we moved to Spain, it was time to welcome back our alpacas. We were nervous, of course, since some of the animals had become ill and died at Peter's farm, but the problem seemed to have passed and our animals had been in isolation away from the animals with the illness.

Our little Rafa was six months old, and had just been weaned from his mother. All our three girls were pregnant, to three different males, and due to give birth later in the year. Rafa had had an x-ray to check all was okay, but there was a suspect shadow on his chest so he was being given antibiotic injections, and we needed to arrange to take him for a follow up x-ray at the local veterinary hospital. Through Manuel, we were able to arrange an appointment and permission to move him for the check-up.

We spent a week trying to train him to walk on a halter so that we would be able to get him to the appointment with no problems. We also had to give him two injections every day, into his muscles, for his antibiotics. This made him very sore and nervous to come to us. It becomes very difficult to thrust a needle into an animal when you know it's causing them obvious pain and discomfort. This was something else we really had not considered when buying the animals. Lots of livestock owners administer their own medicine as it saves on costs, but the first time you have to administer a needle to an animal, it's a horrible experience. Additionally, alpacas, even small ones, are very strong and they can jump as you try to inject.

After his week of injections we were thankful to

finish; we just had to get over the hurdle of the hospital appointment. As he was still pretty small, we managed to load him into the back of our 4x4. He was a bit distraught, but Lorna sat with him and talked to him throughout the journey. We couldn't help but smile to ourselves as cars overtook us. You could see the looks of curiosity as they peered out of their windows whilst passing this beautiful baby alpaca in the back of the car.

When we arrived at the hospital, we were approached immediately by students at the university wanting to touch him and take photos on their phones. We entered the hospital to find 12 students and a number of vets in attendance, all keen to see this strange animal.

Rafa was a star most of the time; he walked through the long corridors on his halter and lead like he was a veteran of the show ring, letting people touch and stroke him. But he did refuse to stand still for the x-ray, so it took a few minutes to get done.

The head vet suggested we take a walk outside for a while, so Rafa could relax and get some fresh air whilst they took their time checking over the x-rays. Students from the university were very curious and again came up to us and asked questions about him.

Thankfully the x-ray turned out to be normal, so we went home happy and breathing a huge sigh of relief. With all three girls now pregnant we decided to try and keep them as stress-free as possible, so for the next few months we didn't handle them unless absolutely necessary. We were definitely paranoid. To this day, if an alpaca is asleep sunbathing, as they like to do, I go and wake them up. I know alpacas like to soak up the sun, particularly ours it seems, but that first year's experiences and the losses we had have affected me and I am always looking for problems.

This new place is a bit of a nightmare. Since we arrived, every day, the people have been sticking needles into me, and it really hurts. I try to move, to tell them it's sore but they keep doing it. Then, yesterday, they bundled me into their car and took me away from Mum, to a place which was full of people and no other alpacas anywhere. There wasn't even a poo pile. All these people were touching me and prodding me, and trying to make me stand still, but I was very nervous. Eventually they stopped trying to pull me about, and after letting even more people touch my fleece, they put me back in the car, and took me home to Mum. I was so glad to see her, and my aunties, that I ran around the field for a few minutes. This seemed to make the people laugh. Anyway I felt much better after some dinner, and a big poo, and hopefully they will leave me alone now so I can play.

Rafa

Chapter 23
Fishing with the Locals

Animal count: Four dogs, three feral cats, one pot-bellied pig, two chickens and four alpacas (Cassandra, Lily, Bermuda and Rafa).

One early spring morning, when the mornings were fresh and sometimes there was even ice on the cars, I was awoken by urgent car horns and shouting outside. Jumping out of bed and throwing on clothes in a hurry in case of a problem with the alpacas, I found Ramon and Miguel outside jabbering and gesturing away to me. They had fishing rods in the truck and wanted me to get in with them. Promises of big fish were made and grand displays of the size of previous catches were implied. They had (lots of) beer with them, and even some Coke for me. In the name of neighbourhood relations, we never know when we may need some help, so I trudged in to see Lorna and said, "I'm going fishing with Ramon and Miguel."

She just laughed. Fishing is not really my thing, and the thought of me sitting on a river bank spending the day with these two characters amused her greatly.

Miguel and Ramon know the area far better than I can ever hope to, having farmed here for the majority of their lives. They have 'discussions' that you always feel are one wrong word away from a full-blown fist fight, but then something amuses the other, and backslapping and laughter is resumed. It's all part of a good, healthy discussion.

We dawdled up the track, on a different course to anywhere Lorna and I had driven, and as we drove up and over the top of a hill there appeared a large lake we had no idea even existed, and it was only five minutes away from our house.

We turned onto a small track, running through a dense, forest laden area, and emerged in a clearing, on the edge of the lake. There was an upturned wooden dinghy at the water's edge. I hadn't really bargained on being trapped in a small boat with these two lunatics, and having seen Miguel's lively performances to date, I just knew we were destined to end up capsized in the water.

Without any further ado, I was ushered to work, helping lift the dinghy into the water.

"*Venga, venga*" and "*mas fuerte*" were being shouted at me. "C'mon, c'mon" and "more strong."

We unloaded the car, and there were some fishing rods, bait, cans of beer, coca-cola and "mucho" stale bread and olive oil in an old cola bottle. Ramon climbed into the boat and we handed him the provisions. In the role befitting the elder gentleman in the group, he then began directing us.

Miguel and I pushed the boat out onto the water, submerging our feet and ankles, and then jumped in the boat, while it rocked wildly from side to side. Ramon and Miguel were in fits of laughter, most the time I never really understand why. I wasn't really sure if this was a serious fishing expedition or a big old laugh at the crazy English bloke's expense. Either way I was entertaining them. We used a long stick as a kind of punt, and propelled ourselves out in to the lake. Miguel, with his customary ear-to-ear grin handed me a rod and then offered me the bait container. I grimaced at him.

"*Nooo, solo mira. Me, no,*" giving a definitive no-way signal with my hands. I was trying to say I was happy just to watch. Of course, this meant more laughter. These Spanish farmers must wonder what I spent my youth doing. I don't know how to fish, or ride a horse, and as for working on the olives, as far as they are concerned I am next to useless.

Ramon and Miguel threw the lines into the water and cracked open the beers. We waited and drank. Drank and waited. After what seemed like an age of nothing happening, although in reality only an hour had passed,

103

both Ramon and Miguel began to drift off to sleep in the bloody boat. After about another 30 minutes, one line twitched slightly, and Miguel was wide awake and alert.

"¡*Zapatilla, zapatilla!*" He was shaking Ramon.

I didn't find out until much later that many of the locals have nicknames for each other. Ramon's nickname was 'Zapatilla'. This translates as slippers, but when they refer to Ramon, it means 'Little Shoes.' It's a tongue in cheek reference to his diminutive height.

Miguel's nickname is 'Pollito' – Little Chicken. There is even a family in Montoro whose nickname translates as 'The Carrots', although we have never managed to find out why they are called that.

Ramon wound in his fishing line, and on the hook was a small, thin fish about twice the size of a stickleback. Ramon had a huge grin on his face. The fish was freed from the hook, and chucked, unceremoniously into a bucket of water. Over the next few hours, Ramon and Miguel got steadily more inebriated, and their discussions became increasingly animated, and often hilarious. At one stage, while reeling in one of the fish that afternoon, Ramon lost his balance, rocking the whole boat and almost coming a cropper in the water. If it hadn't been for Miguel grabbing him by the trousers, he would have been a goner.

By the end of the experience, having caught precisely twelve fish, enough for one of them to have for supper, maybe, and worth less than the cost of the beer they drank, I was punting us back towards the shore. I jumped down near the water's edge and tried to pull it in. But the dinghy was heavy with both the sleepy men in it, so I had to rouse them from their slumbers to jump down from the boat. Miguel jumped down easily, but Ramon was wobbling. I offered him my hand for support. His balance went, and as I struggled to keep him upright, I stumbled forward, losing my footing in the mud, falling head first into the shallow, brown, murky water. Ramon, using my loss of balance, propelled himself gracefully to land. As I stood up, with my face covered in mud and my clothes saturated, my two companions couldn't help but burst out in fits of laughter.

Sometimes I try to imagine the conversations that must go on between the farmers about us. I'm sure they must think we mean well, but I'm pretty sure that in their eyes, we truly are the *Loco Ingles.*

When I returned home, having been driven back along the track at a very slow pace by a tipsy Miguel, I walked into more laughter, this time from Lorna. She had a look on her face that said, "Do I even need to ask?"

Chapter 24
Pregnant? No, of course not!

"I'm not pregnant, Mum. Don't worry, we're always careful. It must be something else." Frankie's voice was coming from the laptop.

"Well, if you don't feel better by the weekend you should check it out, Frankie," Lorna said, with a telling raise of the eyebrows.

For a couple of weeks Frankie had been complaining to her Mum about feeling unwell, and to Lorna, the symptoms sounded suspiciously like early pregnancy. Frankie and Chris had been together for three years and a baby certainly wasn't planned.

"Okay, I promise I will. I'm a bit busy for the next couple of days, but I can do it on Sunday, and then I'll let you know. I'll be phoning anyway, because it's Mother's Day!"

"Okay," Lorna said.

Sunday came around and Lorna was on edge. Hours dragged by, and there was no phone call, and as time passed Lorna knew the result without even speaking to Frankie. The call came on Skype.

"Hi darling, are you okay?"

"Hi Mum. Happy Mother's Day. Yeah I'm fine thanks, how are you?"

All very pleasant.

"I'm fine. Well, did you do it?"

"Yes," Frankie replied sheepishly, before bursting into tears and wailing, "I'm pregnant."

Lorna wasn't totally surprised but as far as she was concerned grandchildren were not really on the horizon in the near future. She had hoped that maybe, with both her children working and settled they would be able to enjoy life a bit, take some nice holidays and then have children later on.

Mark, who was staying with us for a few weeks helping us with some work, looked at me and said with a grin, "I don't think my box of Ferrero Rocher is going to beat that."

"Hmm, I don't think so, Mark."

After the dust settled, and everyone was used to the idea of Frankie becoming a mum, Mark was due to fly home.

Lorna said to him, "Look, I know you want babies one day, but don't rush into anything just because Frankie is pregnant. Enjoy yourself, go on holiday, don't get too tied down."

Mark was in a new relationship, but Lorna knew he yearned for a baby. The advice went in one ear and out of the other.

A few weeks later, Mark phoned to say that his girlfriend, Callie, was pregnant. Frankie was due to give birth in November and Callie in March. Again the question had to be asked now there were grandchildren on the way.

"Do you want to go home? Move back to England for the kids?"

"No," she assured me. "They've got their own lives, they have made their decision to get pregnant. I can still visit, I just have to make sure it's quality time over quantity."

In a way it was lucky it happened as it did: if the babies had come along before we left the UK, Lorna would never have been able to leave.

Chapter 25
A Small World

Animal count: Four dogs, three feral cats, three new feral kittens (We decided now was a good time to start naming the cats. They had grown in number, and the mother was looking thin. We started to feed them a little, especially when she was feeding the new kittens. She also fed the previous year's kittens, too, and we felt this was too much for her, so we tried to help. We named the group after the TV show, The Royal Family, so the Mum was Barb, last year's kittens were Jim and Dave, and the three little babies were R Denise, Twiggy and Baby David). Plus one pot-bellied pig, two chickens and four alpacas.

"We've had an email from a guy called Michael Heath. "He wants to visit us, well everybody here who has alpacas. He's organising a big alpaca conference in Madrid. He wants to come and see us with his partner Ciano."

"Okay," I said, "We'll email him back and tell him he's more than welcome to pop by."

A few weeks later I went out to meet the couple at our regular rendezvous point. I was greeted by two, very well-groomed gentlemen, one Spanish and one English. Coming from Brighton, and having now been in a relationship with Lorna for a number of years, I had become used to meeting gay men. One of her best friends in Brighton was gay, and in the dance world it is very common. However, in Spain, we very rarely see overtly gay men, especially in the small village where we live. In Brighton, it is practically normal to see over-the-top campness on every corner, but Spain is still a very macho country.

We invited Michael and Ciano in for a drink, and

became completely engrossed in talking about alpacas and the conference that Michael was proposing to host in a large hotel in Madrid, all very sensible and business like.

"Why are you holding a conference about alpacas? You don't own any, do you?" I asked Michael.

"Well, I'm by trade, a dealer in animal skins. In fact I used to keep ostriches to breed for the skins, but now I buy, and import and export them all over the world. At the moment alpaca fleece is one of the big markets. I have experience in putting on big conferences, and thought I could make this a success." He paused, and then asked, "What about you two? How did you get into alpacas?"

Normally, at this point, Lorna takes over the story, and starts from the beginning.

"To cut a very long story short, I was a dance teacher for 30 years and I had a few health problems, which started to make things difficult. We decided to change our life, so we headed to Spain, bought this house and decided to breed alpacas."

"Wow," Michael replied. "A dance teacher? I don't believe it." His voice rose excitedly. "Where did you teach? I used to teach dancing too!"

"Noooo, really? Wow, it really is a small world! I used to have a dance school in Brighton."

"Oh my God!" his hands went up to his face. "I used to teach in Brighton too," he said. "Lorna…Lorna," Michael seemed as though he was trying to recall a name. "Lorna Roff. I used to teach for Lorna Roff."

"But that's me! That was my maiden name. I don't believe this, I came to Spain to get away from dancing."

Well, the arms flew in the air and full camp mode was assumed.

"Don't you remember? Michael Heath? I used to teach Latin American dancing for you."

Slowly Lorna began to recall this man who had only taught for her for a few months. They were both about 25 years older and slightly rounder in shape. Of course, when we had received the email, Lorna had never cottoned on, because it was alpaca-related and this man lived in Spain.

Of all the places, in all the world, to run into someone you worked with 25 years before, in a remote Olive Mill in rural Andalucía, talking about alpacas. The odds on that must be astronomical.

Chapter 26
The Lost Goats

The weather started to warm as our second Andalucían summer approached, and we began to receive a few visitors, family and friends wanting to come and experience our new life. Normally we arrange to meet them, and on getting out of the car the first question they tend to ask is, "How did you find this place?" followed by, "Now we understand why you insisted on meeting us!"

Two of our first guests were Karen and Nick, and they were seasoned travellers, having spent two years travelling and working their way around the world. We were waiting for the phone call, as we always do, when suddenly the phone buzzed.

"Hi Karen," Lorna answered.

"Hiya Lorna. We've got a little problem, we are slightly lost."

"Okay, where are you?" she said, thinking they had missed the turning on the motorway or gone wrong at Cordoba.

"Well, we turned off the motorway at your exit, and we thought we would be able to find you. We had seen the pictures on Facebook and there can't be many alpacas around. But we went down a track, and now we have come to a gate that we thought might be yours. There are lots of olive trees around!"

"I'll send Alan out to check, but I don't think you are outside, the dogs normally go mad."

Of course they weren't outside. As they were friends of Lorna, she decided she would go out with the phone and try to find them. After an hour of searching, she managed to get them to retrace their steps and find their way out and stay there for her to find. To this day, we don't really know where they went, or which gate they were sitting outside.

One morning, when Karen and Nick were outside feeding the alpacas and drinking coffee, Karen came running in. "Lorna, Lorna," she rested her hands on her knees to catch her breath. "There are four goats outside looking at the alpacas."

"Oh no, where have they come from?"

The last thing we needed was to adopt some stray goats.

Lorna went out to investigate, and sure enough, there they were, four shy and nervous goats. A little family. We had never seen or heard goats before so Lorna was perplexed.

The next thing she knew was the rattling of an old pick-up truck and the screaming of brakes as Ramon came hurtling around the corner. Ramon jumped out of the passenger side of the car and his son, who was driving, disappeared again back up the track, to open the gate apparently. Ramon encouraged Lorna, and of course Karen and Nick to herd the goats down the track to the river bed and then along in the direction of his house.

"Errr where are we going, Lorna?" Karen whispered, unnecessarily of course as Ramon speaks no English.

"I think he wants us to help him get them back to his house. I think it's only round the corner, it won't take long."

As she was talking, Ramon shouted at her to stop the goats going up the hill, and to keep them moving in the right direction.

As the sun rose higher in the sky, so did the temperature, and the gang of four were sweating. Far from being just around the corner, although the entrance to his Finca was, the house and animal pens were a further three or four kilometres over rough and stony terrain. As they neared the buildings in the distance, a chorus of dogs barking and howling broke out, welcoming their master home. Four small, rough-looking dogs came running out barking and yapping and jumping at Ramon, followed by a great lump of a canine, strolling casually behind.

112

As the house got thankfully closer, there were more dogs, tied to trees to stop them escaping, fighting or breeding, I guess. One part of Spanish rural life we find difficult to deal with is the treatment of dogs, but we are happy that at least they get fed and watered daily at Ramon's, we hear of worse stories elsewhere.

As they approached, Ramon could obviously see Lorna looking sadly at his collection of mutts, and seizing his opportunity, he tried to offer her the pick of the bunch, any one she wanted. Knowing I would not be happy with another addition to our brood, she had to be strong and decline the offer.

The goats were ushered into a pen fashioned from a selection of old wooden pallets, held together by wire and pieces of baling twine. Ramon disappeared into the ramshackle old building adjacent to the pen. He emerged with a beautiful, tiny white rabbit and presented it to Lorna. She took it in her arms, instantly falling in love, but knowing we had nowhere to keep it. Reluctantly, she handed it back, hoping and praying that one day it didn't end up skinned and presented to us for dinner!

Lorna was ushering the group out of the house as they were in a hurry to get back so Karen and Nick could get on the road; they had a plane to catch. Ramon's son, Ramon, offered them a lift. We see him go past most days in his (surprise, surprise) battered old pick-up truck, and he drives at a considerable rate of knots. Lorna was holding on tight as he rounded the bends and even drove through an uneven, rocky river, where the occupants were thrown about like ping-pong balls in a bingo machine. Karen and Nick made their flight by the skin of their teeth.

Chapter 27
The Happiest Dog in the World

The final addition to our dog pack came at the end of our second summer in the Olive Mill.

"Bloody hell, Arthur's going ballistic out there, Alan!"

Taking that as my cue, I went to check it out. "Okay, I'll have a look."

I looked out of the window, expecting to see a cat or another animal tormenting him just by being there, but I couldn't see anything. Arthur was still carrying on as though something was wrong, so I went and looked out of the gate.

"Uh-oh!" I thought to myself and went back in to Lorna.

"Erm, it's a puppy," I grimaced. "It's only small, I'm going to try to put him back out, under the gate, see if goes home or off somewhere else. Don't come out," I added, knowing that if she did, and she saw the pup, she would want to keep him.

I ushered him back under the gate and blocked it with some wood we had lying around, and went back in, hoping that he would find a different place to live. It can't have been more than 30 seconds later when Arthur started again. I knew he had got back in.

"I'll come out with you this time," Lorna said.

"Are you sure?" I checked. "You know we can't have any more dogs, we don't really cope with the ones we already have."

"I know," Lorna replied dismissively.

As we neared the gate, a little bundle of brown energy came running over to us, shaking his bum, and looking at us with love in his eyes. He had big floppy ears, far too big for his head, and he was about the size of a small cat. It was hot, so we gave him a drink and a little food.

"Well, I guess we could keep him in the stable for a couple of days, see if anyone comes looking for him, and then go from there." I suggested, knowing in my head that this one could be a keeper. So that's what we did. Over a few days we noticed that the puppy didn't move well; he walked with a limp. One of his back legs was particularly weak, and although he didn't seem to be in pain, it definitely wasn't normal.

We took him to see Manuel, to ask about the leg and to check if there could be a microchip with details of an owner on it. Of course there wasn't. Manuel examined the dog, and explained that he thought, possibly, that he had been hit by a car or something large, causing his hip to become dislocated and causing a few minor abrasions on his body. "I think it will need an operation," he said apologetically.

I looked at Lorna. Lorna looked back at me.

Lorna said, "No one is going to pay for an operation for him, maybe we could get that sorted for him."

I sighed. "If we are going to pay for the operation, we may as well keep him."

Lorna smiled.

"Why don't you see how he gets on for a while," Manuel said. "He will need his vaccinations in a few weeks, we can talk about the operation later."

So off we went, and one less stray dog roamed the campo in Andalucía.

A year had gone since we acquired Blue and Arthur, and to be honest we hadn't really got to grips with them. They were not very good on leads, either far too strong for us, or refusing to move and just lying in the road. We were also scared of Geri getting hurt by their sheer size, so we had separated them into pairs: Geri with Carlos, Blue with Arthur. It wasn't ideal, but we didn't really know how to deal with such strong dogs.

Gradually we began to introduce the puppy to the other dogs, firstly Blue and Arthur. Blue went crazy, playing like a giant puppy, paws on the ground, head down and bottom in the air, with her small, stumpy tail wagging to and fro. We were worried the puppy would get hurt, and a few times he got trod on, or bashed too hard and he whimpered a little, but then he was quickly back up and in the faces of his new friends once again. They were like three little children who had just found each other.

We then tried to take him through to meet the smaller dogs.

"I'll hold the big two, while you open the gate and take him through," I suggested.

The picture I had in my head went much smoother than the reality.

Pandemonium ensued. The two big dogs pulled me to the ground, but I tried to hold on.

"Quickly close the gate!" I called from my now horizontal position. Lorna turned to see why I was in distress, and that was all they needed; Blue and Arthur pulled away from me, and the puppy jumped from Lorna's arms. The puppy was in the faces of all the dogs, Geri was barking, and Carlos, normally so quiet, joined in too.

We had been advised by a dog-breeder friend of ours to put all the dogs in together, shut the door, and not to return for 15 minutes - however bad it sounds, they will sort it out. So, knowing no other option, that is what we did. We really had no alternative. After 15 minutes, of what sounded like hell on earth, quiet suddenly descended and everything went silent. We looked out and order had been established – ish. All the dogs had retreated to different shady corners, and the puppy was busy going from corner to corner, trying to be friends with all the others. To be honest he had done us a favour, he had brought our band of individuals together. We now had our pack!

The little fella, it turns out, may be a distant relative of a cat as he seems to have nine lives. We named him Miliko, after a misunderstanding involving the name of a famous Spanish clown Miliki, but we liked Miliko, and it seems to suit him.

A few days later we woke to find him severely unwell. He wouldn't eat, wouldn't drink and wouldn't come out from under a chair. We were really worried about him, so whipped him back up to the vets. Manuel said that he was vulnerable as he was not yet ready for his injections and of course he was mixing with the other dogs now. He had caught an infection, and if we hadn't brought him in it could have been fatal. For a week, we had to syringe feed him baby penicillin, and he became our baby.

He recovered well, and as he got stronger we began to notice he was using the problem back leg even less. He could climb steps, but he would use his front legs to pull himself up so his front leg muscles became super strong. We now needed to get the operation sorted or later on it might become an issue for him.

The operation was to be done in Cordoba – they even drafted in an extra English-speaking vet to be there to translate for us. We took Miliko in and, after running in and out of every room in the surgery, he was lifted onto the scales and his blood was checked. Then, we expected to leave him with them, possibly overnight, while the operation and recovery took place. Not at all, we were ushered into the operating theatre where we discovered we were expected to be present right until he was asleep, and had to return before he was brought round so he felt as though we'd always been there.

On our return, the vet was very serious. When they had tried to put a tube down his mouth, to help him breathe during the operation, they found that he was unable to open his mouth properly. They had to break his jaw to get the tube in, therefore he was going to be sore for a few days. Where he had been hit by the car, his jaw had been broken and reset itself in the wrong place.

Once he came around, we carried him out to the car and wrapped him in a blanket for the journey. We carried him in to the house and let him sleep on the sofa for a couple of hours. That evening he was very sorry for himself, and he wouldn't eat. We put him back to bed, with his big mate Arthur, and went off to bed. First thing in the morning I got up, thinking I might need to carry him out for a wee, but the blanket was on the floor and Miliko was doing an excited tour of the living room, jumping on both sofas and at me, obviously wanting to go out. All of this on three legs! He wasn't even trying to use the leg that had been operated on.

I thought then, "It's going to be tough to keep him still for a few days." Even today he still bears his battle scars: his one bad leg is significantly shorter than the other and he cannot open his mouth more than 18 millimetres. He eats very slowly and gets frustrated, and in the summer we only take him for short walks because he cannot put his tongue out and open his mouth to pant like a normal dog. However, he is a very happy dog, even having been described as the happiest dog in the world.

When they put me under that fence, I knew I was meant to be here. I could see a friendly face immediately. There was a big boy calling to me, saying he wanted to be friends.

Eventually a person came outside, I think the other dog told him I was here, and he looked at me and tried to tell me to go away. He put me under the fence, but I just came back in anyway. I liked this place and I wanted to stay.

Then a lady came out too, and they gave me some water and a little food, and they let me sleep in their stable for a few days. They took me to the doctor, and looked at my legs, I think they are going to let me stay. I was so desperate to meet the other dog and one day they let him out to meet me. He is very big but I'm not scared of him, he's a big softy. His sister came out too, and she seems scary; she keeps trying to play with me, but she bashes me and I just go flying. She is so much bigger than me. Anyway, I managed to get in one day and meet the other two as well, one of them is really grumpy, but I think she likes me in a way.

It's all very exciting and I can't wait to see them all every day to play with them all over again.
Miliko

Chapter 28
Galaxy

Animal count: Five dogs (Geri, Carlos, Blue, Arthur and Miliko), one feral cat and one feral kitten. (I had always worried that the cats would just multiply into hundreds of cats around the farm, but this year the two older cats, and two of the kittens, Twiggy and Baby David,vanished together. We never knew if they had been taken by an eagle or if they had been sent on their way by their Mum. She was left with just one kitten, and she was able to manage far better.) One pot-bellied pig, two chickens, four alpacas.

"I think I'd better go and check on Cassandra," I said to Lorna. "I've just looked out the window and she looks a little agitated." We had been watching closely for weeks now, anxiously awaiting the birth of the first cria on our own farm. "I don't think it's going to be long now."

As I walked around to the paddock, I mentally checked off what we would need, "Clean towel, iodine spray, scissors, alpaca book, phone!" When I arrived at the gate, I could immediately see Cassandra's 'area' swollen, and she was visibly straining.

"It's happening now!" I shouted through the window, running off to get the birthing equipment.

"But it's only supposed to happen in the mornings!" was Lorna's first reaction.

"Well, tell that to Cassandra!" I yelled, my stomach turning somersaults, and adrenalin flowing.

We grabbed everything we could, luckily all to hand, as we had been told to prepare, and on our return to the paddock, we opened our alpaca book, hoping it would be, as they say, a textbook delivery.

"The book says, 'Mother will show signs of distress,

119

frequent visits to the poo pile without going, and separating herself from the others.'"

"She's doing all of that," Lorna replied. "I think this is really it! What do we do now?"

"Wait, I guess. The book says, if all goes correctly, she will do it on her own, and the head should emerge first, quickly followed by the two front legs. Please God, it comes out the right way."

Sure enough, on the next visit to the pile, there was more pushing, a noticeable widening of the vagina and something popped out.

"What is it?" Lorna asked. "Is it the head?" The birthing sack was yet to burst.

"Oh my God, should we split it?" I panicked.

"Wait a minute," Lorna replied calmly.

With a loud gush, the bag split, and a little head and mouth could be seen gasping its first little breaths, followed quickly by two little feet.

"Thank God for that, at least it's the right way round!" I breathed a little sigh of relief, but we were not home and dry yet.

"The book says, 'A normal delivery should take between five and 20 minutes, and she may stand, walk, sit down or lie down during this time.'"

Cassandra was obviously uncomfortable and she was wandering around, eating a little, lying down, standing up and all this time the poor little baby was swinging about, brushing up against the wall and gradually slipping out, closer and closer to the ground. With a final push, the tiny little alpaca thumped to the earth. A solid, dark, chocolatey brown-coloured cria. Beautiful.

"Oh wow, how amazing was that?" Lorna exclaimed with tears in her eyes.

"Look at the others, they're going to say hello."

One by one, the other girls and Rafa all had a good sniff of the new arrival. Almost in celebration, Rafa jumped excitedly about.

We rushed in, dried the cria off with the towel, and sprayed the umbilical cord to prevent infection. We checked the sex, and it was a boy. Then we stood back and watched. The next part is often the most frustrating for alpaca breeders, as it is very important the new baby receives the first milk from its mother within a short amount of hours. This time is often spent watching closely and holding your breath every time the baby gets near to the mother's milk.

Such was the paranoia and nervousness brought on by our bad experiences in our short time as alpaca owners, there are photographs of the new cria with me in the background studying the alpaca book, making sure every last detail was okay.

Within a few minutes, the cria had found his feet, stumbling around and falling on his face numerous times. Cassandra is a very independent mother, and her first thought after the birth was to get herself a feed. So the poor little cria was stumbling along behind her, looking dazed and confused, then sat down for a while to rest. We sighed. More waiting.

"Here he goes again," Lorna said. "Good luck, little fella."

This time there was a more concerted effort. The feet were a little steadier, and he was heading in roughly the right direction. With a little nudge from Cassandra he eventually found the milk and we could relax, at least for a while. We came away from the paddock to allow the new little family to bond. Our first alpaca birth was indeed textbook, and exhilarating, and hopefully the little man would grow up to be big and strong.

"We need a name now," I said to Lorna.

"Well, he is that gorgeous colour, why don't we call him Galaxy?"

"Not very Spanish, is it?" I replied.

"Nope, but I like it."

"Okay, Galaxy it is!"

Over the next few days and weeks, we monitored Galaxy's weight; he was putting on more and more and was feeding well, so we were happy. Now we could begin to get excited about the next babies. Lily and Bermuda were due to have their cria around Christmas, and we were hoping for more of the same from our girls.

Chapter 29
Feria Time

Animal count: Five dogs, one feral cat, one feral kitten, one pot-bellied pig, two chickens, five alpacas (Cassandra, Lily, Bermuda, Rafa and now Galaxy).

Initially we would shy away from situations where we might run into difficulty with our truly inept Spanish, but in the run up to the local *Feria* in Montoro in October, we had promised both Miguel and Ramon that we would attend the fair. Although we were nervous, knowing that they would be there, helped a little.

So one night we headed off into Montoro, leaving home at about 10 pm. There was no moon in the sky; everything was pitch black. As we reached the top of our track, our headlights picked up something moving ahead of us. Both of our first instincts were 'stray dog' but we were wrong. In fact there was a family of wild boar crossing the road, two adults and a few youngsters. We were really pleased as they were the first we had ever seen since we had moved here.

We drove on to Montoro and had to park the car a few hundred metres away from the *Feria* ground, as of course the town was heaving and in full party mode. The *Feria* is the second biggest event of the year in most Spanish villages, only beaten by the Easter celebrations in this still staunchly Catholic country. Montoreños from all over Andalucía and beyond come home for the party.

The roads were decked out with illuminated decorations stretching from one side to the other, along with suspect-looking wiring hanging from the sides of houses.

As we walked up the road, we could hear loud music playing and lots of frivolity. We entered the fairground, and the place was heaving: hundreds of people standing shoulder to shoulder, inching their way from place to place. At one end of the ground was a large fair, complete with rides and sideshows.

To our distress, also there was a live animal merry-go-round with miniature donkeys and horses. Although the animals looked in good condition it was not nice for us to see, as they should be out in a field somewhere grazing on lush grass. The other end of the ground was dedicated to the *casetas*, tents run by various companies and bars which host people for drinks, music and food. As we walked around, we were astonished to see *churros* stalls (a kind of Spanish donut), cooking the local delicacy in vats of boiling hot fat, only three feet off of the ground and easily within reach of any of the hundreds of children in attendance. In the UK, the health and safety people would have had it shut down in seconds.

There were crazy big rides, like the large disc where people take seats around the edge, with no restraints, and then proceed to get thrown around, eventually falling into a heap of bodies on the floor. This particular ride seems to be used by teenage boys and girls as an excuse to end up on the floor together.

Of course one of the highlights of any *Feria*, in any town, is to see the locals in their traditional gypsy clothes, often dancing the night away, or with children in their best clothes on the dodgems.

"So where do we go now?" I asked.

"I'm not sure, maybe we could have a look in a few of the bars, see if we can find Miguel or Ramon?" Lorna suggested.

Suddenly, we could hear shouting and booming laughter, and we didn't need to look very far, as we could recognise Miguel's voice from a hundred yards.

We followed the voice into one of the tents and found Miguel holding court, surrounded by a clutch of familiar looking older gentlemen, probably farmers, and a few 'handsome' women.

A space was made for us and we were welcomed into

the crowd, drinks were ordered, and I was, as usual, laughed at. A fiesta like this also calls for food, and lots of it, and Miguel was doing the honours. At times like this the Spanish like to order big plates of food to go into the middle and be shared out tapas style. I could make out a few words, '*Cerdo*' is pork, '*Pollo*' is chicken and '*Cabritos*' is baby goat. There was also Spanish omelette, *Pinchitos* (Chicken skewers), *Flamenquin* (Spanish pork and ham rolled in batter), cured ham and cheese, calamari, baby squid and of course plates of chips and stale bread.

There was food everywhere and the farmers dove in wholeheartedly, while Lorna and I were a little more reserved, picking at a few morsels here and there. The drink flowed continuously, and of course much of the conversation passed us by completely. Occasionally we would pick up a word or phrase we might recognise or be able to contribute, but most of the time we nodded and laughed when it seemed most appropriate.

After numerous drinks and lots of laughter, one of the wives got up all of a sudden, as though she had been possessed by the music, and began to dance. Her eyes were closed, hands in the air, fingers clicking, heels clacking and twirling for all she was worth. Miguel and his friends were soon dancing too (Miguel was keen to drag Lorna up, and although she made a show of fighting it, secretly I think she was dying to join in).

After a few minutes and drink or two more Lorna was stamping, clicking and twirling with the rest of them. After a couple of songs, there was a kerfuffle, a discussion and the group shuffled out en masse, and headed towards the fairground rides. We didn't know where we were going, or indeed why everyone seemed to be having such a laugh.

We ended up standing in front of two plastic bulls, attached to two long rubber logs, and the idea was to sit on the log while it rolled from side to side, and the people on board try in vain to stay on. There was no way Miguel was going to let me off this one, so I had to sit on the log, between Miguel and a couple of ageing farmers that we see drive past our farm once in a while. Some of the farmers were so drunk their eyes were crossed, and to be perfectly frank, half of them didn't even put out their cigarettes.

The ride started moving, slowly at first, and one old boy, slowly, so slowly, just slid to the padded floor with his cigarette still in his mouth and never got back up. I'm sure he fell asleep there. Then as the ride got faster people were thrown into heaps on the floor, hilarity ensued, a few injuries were received, and then you had to climb back on. I think that ride is much more for the entertainment of the people watching than for the people on the ride. My main target was not to land on any frail old men and hurt them. Lorna's main target was trying not to wet herself.

At the end of the ride Miguel was laughing, as per usual, but the rest of the farmers walked off as though they had just left work, straight-faced and non-smiling. Very strange. Then of course it was back to a different tent for more drinking, more food and more music. All this continued until about six in the morning. Then they expect you to go and have churros and chocolate with them; it never ends. We were exhausted, but they wanted us back again that night for more of the same. We politely declined. The Montoro Feria lasts for six days and most of the people attend every day, and then again at night. I'm not really sure how they survive.

Chapter 30
Kaci's Birth, Lily's Loss

As you might expect, Lorna wanted to be in the UK for the birth of her first grandchild, and Frankie wanted her there too, possibly during the birth. We booked some flights, aiming for a couple of days before the due date, hoping Frankie could keep her legs crossed until then. Lorna wanted to be there for at least a couple of weeks to help Frankie through those tough first days.

As normally happens when Lorna is away, all hell let loose on the farm. Although we have never felt scared or nervous living this far from civilisation, sometimes the isolation can be eerie, particularly at night when there is no one around for miles. You find yourself scrutinising every little sound, just in case it might be an intruder. Thank goodness for giant guard dogs!

On the first day of Lorna's absence, two strangers arrived, hollering outside the front gate. They were 'Romanos', Romanian workers here for the olive harvest. Through over-exaggerated gestures, I managed to understand they had a problem with their car and wanted me to tow them up the hill. So I jumped in trusty old Frank (the car had got the nickname Frank from his FNK number plate, and he had been trusty for over a year now), and drove to their car. I then understood the problem. They had got stuck, halfway up the hill, on the wet mud caused by the first of the winter rains. Their tyres couldn't get a grip, so I dragged them, slipping and sliding up to the top of the hill, and sent them off. With a gracious wave and a smile they leaned out of the window "Adioooo, Mucha Graciaaaa!"

The following night, I was happily ensconced in our small apartment with all the dogs settled on various settees and chairs around the room. Everything was silent and I was reading under the dim glow of an energy saving light bulb. All of a sudden the dogs were barking and clawing at the windows and doors desperate to be let out. In this situation, whoever you are, your instinct is that someone is outside. So I tried to shut the dogs up, and listened carefully. There was a scratching coming from outside the window, so my first thought was, "Oh no, we've got rats", but, as I looked out of the window, a little face pulled itself up. There was one of this year's little feral kittens staring up at me. Thinking that they should know better than to come in to the dogs' area, I opened the door of the apartment to scare the cat away and to teach it a lesson. The dogs are never quick enough to get close to the cats anyway.

But this cat was different, it shot off in the wrong direction, scrambling up a brickwork pillar and fell headfirst into our water deposit. There were, in fact, two kittens, the other one huddled down flat on top of the wall, out of the reach of the dogs. I managed to drag the baying dogs back into the apartment, grabbed the kittens and threw them through the iron gates at the end of the terrace.

I then let the dogs out again and went to investigate. These cats were not our own, although they looked remarkably similar to two of our kittens. They were a little smaller and a little more nervous. Someone had obviously dumped them here on the gullible English. I was fuming, there were already six feral cats living here and I had always had a fear of becoming overrun by wild cats as we cannot get close enough to the female to get her spayed. So I made the regrettable and horrible decision to take the kittens, under cover of darkness, and let them go at the top of the track. I very much hope they survived, and I am not proud of doing it, but we have come to realise that as much as we would like to, we just cannot save every animal out there.

People always say these things happen in threes. The next night, after weeks of excitement, I was due to play my first game of football in two years, in the town of Montoro. My friend had asked me to play for his team, and I was excited. Although it was raining hard, I got myself ready and headed out, but by the time I got to the top of the track David called me to say that because it was raining, he wouldn't be going. No-one plays in the rain apparently. So I turned the car around and, driving back down the track, the headlights started to dim and flash. I was a bit worried and crawled Frank back to the house, turned the key and tried to switch him back on again. Nothing. Dead. The battery had gone. I managed to get Good Samaritan Keith to come out and change the battery, but the alternator was kaput and the car could only be used during daylight without the lights. At least now I could relax, my three things had all happened, surely nothing else could go wrong during this trip?

On the 15th November, late at night, the mobile phone beeped into life and there was a text message from Lorna to say that Frankie had started her labour but it had been very slow, and she would keep me updated when she had any news.

I woke up early the following morning, anxious to find out if everything was okay, but there were no text messages or missed calls, so I was in the dark about how things were going. I gazed out of the window, wondering what to do with myself now I was up and about so early, and to my surprise Lily was sitting down casually eating, next to a little fawn cria.

"Oh bloody hell."

We were not expecting her baby to come until around Christmas, so I rushed out to see if everything was okay. I dried the baby off, checked the sex, a girl, and sprayed the umbilical cord. I weighed her and she seemed to be a decent weight. I stepped back and watched and waited, hoping for that much needed first feed to occur. The new arrival seemed strong and was making a gallant attempt at her first steps. While I was out attending to mother and baby, the mobile phone rang.

"Hi," I answered, knowing it was Lorna.

"Hiya. Guess what? I'm a Nanny! Frankie had a little girl, early this morning. She had a really tough time, but everything is okay. I'm so proud of her."

"Wow," I said, "congratulations! I'm so pleased, I was a little worried when I hadn't heard anything for a long time. You will never guess what though...Lily has had her baby!"

"Oh my God, she shouldn't have had it until Christmas. They must have been born about the same time. How amazing! Is it alright?"

"It seems to be. It's a little girl, fawn colour, she is beautiful. I'm just out now watching her to make sure she feeds, then I'll go in," I said. "And by the way, I think we are going to have to call this little one Frankie, don't you?"

"Sounds good," said Lorna. And we hung up.

For the next three days, all seemed to be progressing well. I had seen the baby feeding and, although she hadn't gained much weight, they often lose on the first day and she was still the same as the first time I weighed her so I wasn't overly worried. On her fourth day, however, I looked out of the window and saw the cria sitting on the ground; her Mum was up and about feeding, so it didn't quite seem right. I went outside and found that she was shivering, took her temperature and found it to be dangerously low. I got on the phone immediately.

"Hi Penny, it's Alan," I said nervously. "Sorry to be a pain, but Lily had her baby four days ago, but now the baby is very weak and really cold, I don't really know what to do."

"You need to get her warmed up Alan, use warm water and a hot water bottle, you need to get her core temperature up as soon as possible."

I rushed about in real panic mode, grabbing the things I needed and then gently picking up the cria and taking her inside, into the warm. Lily was distraught, humming loudly at me, while I took her baby away. I wrapped the baby in a towel, and started running her a warm bath and heating up some water for a bottle. I called Keith yet again, asking a big favour to see if he could bring the vet to my house because I didn't want to leave the cria. Yet again he came through.

When Manuel arrived he looked nervous; he felt it was important to try and get some fluid into her, but the problem we have with alpacas is that the veins can be notoriously difficult to locate for the vet, especially one with very little alpaca experience. Eventually a vein was located and we managed to get some fluid and a shot of antibiotics into her. Then we had to wait. Manuel said he would get his wife to bring him back later in the day to check on her. In the meantime, I was to keep her warm and keep the fluid going. After a few hours, and when Manuel returned, we found she had gone downhill. Again I phoned Penny to get some more advice.

"Alan it's up to you. You could try taking her to Cordoba Veterinary Hospital and we could meet you there with some alpaca blood plasma, which could be her only chance, otherwise I think you will lose her. Or you could let her go quietly."

I was distraught, on my own, with Lorna in England. I didn't know what to do but made the decision to go for it; if there was a chance of saving her, I wanted her to have it, so I loaded her into the car and arranged to meet Peter and Penny at the hospital. Again they put themselves out for us, and again I was truly grateful.

In the car, driving on the track, it was all I could do to stop myself from bursting in to tears. My stomach was churning and I had a horrible sickly feeling. Everything that we had dreamed of seemed to be going wrong, we didn't seem to be able to get anything right.

On my arrival at the hospital, I was hurried in to a horse treatment area and vets started attending to the cria. As I watched them I knew it was a lost cause: there was a sense of panic and Penny was yet to arrive with the plasma. After a few minutes, and a last little bit of fight, the little cria gave up and she was gone.

We will never know if she had got the plasma if it would have made a difference, or if it was just not meant to be. But whenever I think about it, I always have 'what ifs' in my mind. Was it something I did wrong? Ten minutes later Peter and Penny arrived but I had to tell them it was too late. They were devastated.

"I'm really very sorry Alan, it's not meant to be like this." Penny said as she hugged me.

"Okay, no more hugs, I don't think I can cope with it," I had to say.

On my return home, I went to feed the girls and Lily ran up to me with an almost pleading look in her eyes, and humming loudly, "Where is my baby?" For days and weeks she came up to me with the same look and it broke my heart every time.

Over the next few days, I felt a growing sense of regret at our hasty decision to move to Andalucia, and as the winter rain started to set in, discovered our problems were only just beginning. The kitchen that Neil had fitted and repaired, plus the newly-built living space both started to leak profusely. When it rains here, it really does rain, big heavy drops of rain, that bounce off surfaces and settle, then seep through any gaps or cracks it can find. Our floors were covered in water and I had to wear wellington boots inside.

I tried to speak to Neil but his phone number wasn't working and his e-mail had gone dead. His Facebook page had been deleted, and I had no way of getting in touch with him. I did manage to get hold of Caroline, and she told me he had gone to England to work for a few weeks but she would get him to call us when he returned.

So, our alpaca ideas were not exactly going well, and now, all the money we had poured into the work on the Olive Mill, looked to have been given away to a cowboy. I was fuming, upset and dreading Lorna's return to Spain when I would have to tell her all about it. Of course I kept her up to date with the basics, but I knew I would need to relive everything again on her return. Whilst I know Lorna was having a lovely time in England with Frankie and the new baby, I understood it must have been difficult for her, knowing I was here and struggling.

After nearly three weeks of being a grandmother Lorna finally returned. The rain had stopped for a while and I had managed to clean up the mess, but Lily was still distraught, and I wasn't sure that I wanted to be here anymore. I burst into tears in Lorna's arms, blaming myself for coming up with the idea of moving here and wondering if we had done the right thing.

"If you want to, we can sell up and go home. I don't know what we will do if we do go home, but if that's what you want to do, we will do it," Lorna said to me.

"Well, maybe we should put the house on the market; we can always decide if we want to go home if we can sell it," I replied.

Then we just stood, holding each other and crying for what seemed like hours.

Chapter 31
The Wettest Winter

A lifetime of grey skies and rain could not have prepared us for what was to come next: the wettest Andalucían winter in living memory. One night we were woken during the night by the loudest clap of thunder I have ever experienced. The whole place shook, and the lightning bolts outside lit up the landscape in flashes of brilliance.

Then the rain started, and boy did it come down. We could hear it bouncing on the cobblestones in the courtyard and, as time went on, we could hear the water gushing from the tiles on the roof and running in torrents down the terraces. The dogs were nervous as the storm seemed to settle in between the hills and immerse us in its grip for the next 40 minutes. Eventually the storm moved away although we could still hear the rain coming down. We managed to get back to sleep until morning.

We rose early, expecting to see the clear blue skies once more, but the rain was still sheeting down. On opening the front door, it was clear that the storm had done some damage. Outside we had a nectarine tree we had planted on our arrival at the house, and we had just started to collect fruit from it that last summer. The tree, however, had been a casualty of the high winds whipped up by the storm.

The dogs went out to investigate and started to bark. It was then we noticed that there was a tree on fire. At the edge of our boundary was a large pine tree, sitting serenely on the top of the hill overlooking the landscape. Obviously, during the night, it had been struck by lightning and was ablaze despite the heavy rain that continued to fall. The tree smouldered for a week, even in the rain.

There was a loud noise, coming from the bottom of

our land where we have a meandering little stream which dries up in summer, but does give us the sound of running water for most of the year. That morning, I climbed onto the high walls surrounding the courtyard to see where the noise was coming from. To my surprise, what was a small stream had, overnight, become what can only be described as a fast flowing river. Until this time, we had only seen the stream, at its highest, about two metres wide and only a matter of inches deep. That morning, the river had swelled to about five metres wide and about a metre deep, and was flowing rapidly. The noise was similar to that of a white-water rafting river.

For the next few weeks, the weather persisted: steady rain and occasional storms, daily mopping up from the leaking roof and yet, still no news from Neil or Caroline about fixing the damage. We were living in rubber boots and always seemed to be wearing damp clothes. The alpacas were miserable, always wet, and the dogs hated it as much as we did.

We lay in bed at night listening to the rain continuing to fall. Some nights storms would settle in the hills again, and the next morning the river would have swelled slightly higher. By this time, the water had nearly reached the height of the little bridge that we had to cross to reach the house. The water in the river must have been between nine and ten metres wide, and at least four metres deep in places. The volume of water was incredible.

The local farmers were having a terrible olive season as the storms had dislodged much of the fruit from the trees, thus reducing the harvest by a massive percentage. As we neared the week before Christmas, we had a let-up for a day when the sun managed to break through again. The farmers took immediate advantage of this and started to pick what crops they could, as quickly as possible. Tractors were out and about, people chatting and whacking the trees, and the hills were a hive of activity. Large metal containers were strewn about to collect the tons of olives they were hoping to collect.

Well, two days later, it proved to be a false dawn as,

once again, we were deluged by one of the huge storms. This time, however, was different: as one storm passed, another would roll in to take its place. We battened down the hatches, shut ourselves in and waited it out. I was gazing out of the window, watching the rising water level in the river as this time it breached the top of the bridge and started flowing over the road and washing away the stone and mud holding it in place.

The next thing I knew, one of the large metal containers, half full of olives, was picked up and carried along by the water before lodging itself in the bridge gap, pushing the water around it. The road was impassable, and the mass of water was causing huge amounts of damage. After about ten minutes, slowly, ever so slowly, the corrugated metal tube that makes up the bridge started to lift, and seconds later was being washed down river.

"Oh my God, the bridge has just washed away," I called out to Lorna.

"What do you mean?"

"Come and look, the bridge has gone."

It meant we couldn't get out. How long would it be before it was fixed? It was Christmas week after all, and we would need to get out sooner or later.

Within an hour there was a delegation of farmers congregating where the bridge should be, obviously deciding on a course of action. Some had animals to look after, and some had extra people in their houses, for the olive picking season. After much to-ing and fro-ing, it looked like a decision had been reached, as a man marched back to his truck.

"There is a man with a chainsaw now, I'm not sure what's happening." I was giving a commentary. "Okay, it looks like they are cutting down a eucalyptus tree. Yep, definitely."

"Why?" said Lorna.

"I'm not really sure. It's fallen across the river, and now there is a man cutting off small parts of the top, to flatten it. I think it's to walk across."

"Really? I don't like the sound of that."

136

An older farmer crossed the log on his bottom, but most walked across with no problems.

"Well, we've enough food for a couple of days, I'm sure they'll fix it pretty soon," I said hopefully.

We reached Christmas Eve and no one had yet come out to fix the bridge, and we had run out of food, so we arranged to borrow a friend's car. I set out to cross the makeshift bridge and walk the three kilometres of track, mostly up a steep hill, to meet our friend. I was nervous stepping onto the fallen tree, with the water passing rapidly beneath my feet, but I held my nerve and set off on my mission.

After meeting our friend and getting the car, I managed to pick up some shopping, and head back home. At least we now had a means of getting out, should we need to. No-one was going to be coming out over Christmas and, as the rain eased slightly, the water level in the river started to gradually drop - so much so that by Boxing Day, farmers were beginning to risk driving through the river.

We didn't yet feel ready to risk driving through the river so, the day after Boxing Day, Lorna and I set out to cross the makeshift bridge and spend the day in Cordoba. We were fed up with the weather and the lack of solar electricity; we needed some time out. I had already been across the tree twice so I went across first, and then Lorna started her journey, stepping out nervously, initially, before getting more confident, perhaps a little too confident.

As Miguel passed by on his tractor, Lorna for some strange reason started to do a little dance on the log. A little over-excited at the prospect of going out maybe? When she finished laughing and dancing, she made to move again and found that she couldn't: she had lost her nerve completely. I was laughing at her, thinking she was joking, but she was stuck. Miguel came over to be her knight in shining armour, stepped on the log, and took her hand guiding her to the safety of the river bank. How embarrassing!

At least now we were able to go out and enjoy our day

away from the countryside. However, as with all things Lorna and Alan, it did not go according to plan. Unused to driving the big lump of a pickup truck we had borrowed, I misjudged a pothole in the road caused by the heavy rain, and caught it hard. "BANG!" went the tyre, and I momentarily lost control of the car. I pulled over to the side of the road to discover a great tear in the tyre. We were stuck, about five kilometres from home, and more from town. There was a spare tyre but the tools were missing to do the job.

Guess who we had to call? Yep, you bet, Keith again. Keith came out with his tools and changed the tyre for us, but we had lost so much time we just decided to go back home and have some lunch. What a fab Christmas this was turning out to be.

As we headed into January there was still no let-up in the rain, and we were feeling pretty depressed about life in general. Even the birth of Eduardo, Bermuda's first cria with us, did little to brighten our spirits. He was strong and healthy and all went well, but with the lack of sunlight he did have a slight Vitamin D deficiency, thus making him walk in an unusual manner for a few weeks. However the problem was easily solved with some Vitamin D paste we were able to administer.

Of course, we live with electricity powered only by solar energy so, during that winter, when there was no sun, we had no power. We managed to have a little during daylight hours, but we usually used up our supply by about midnight. We were reading by candlelight and going to bed early. Plus, we were also unable to do any washing so we were wearing the same clothes for days on end, providing we could keep them dry. If they got wet, they went into a pile in the corner. We just hoped one day soon the sun would come out.

Up until now, I had been true to my word and the dogs we had rescued were outside dogs, and only our ageing Geri was allowed the privilege of sleeping in the apartment. This, however, changed one day when the time came for the boys, Arthur and Carlos (although not

138

Miliko, due to his mouth problems), to have the snip. We decided it would better for Manuel to come to the house, and we could do them both together. Arthur was now so big and strong, it was impossible to get him into the car due to his travel sickness. We collected Manuel, but were surprised to see he had no-one with him; we were expecting someone to assist him with the castrations. It turned out, that person was going to be me.

After giving Arthur his pre-anaesthetic, he started to stumble around after a few minutes, and it was time to give him the second injection. When he was fast asleep we heaved him up onto the table, and Manuel told me to hold Arthur's legs apart, as wide as possible. As Manuel made the cut with his scalpel I suppressed the urge to cringe, but I couldn't look away. It was like a car crash. Slowly Manuel popped out the testicles, one by one, made the necessary cuts and then discarded them in a plastic bag. After being stitched back up, Arthur was laid on the ground, and then it was the turn of Carlos.

The same procedure, although Carlos was much easier to manoeuvre around, and soon I had collected four testicles in a plastic bin liner. I put them on the side to deal with later, and went out to take Manuel home. We had decided that the boys could recover inside for the night, then they would have to go back to living outside the following day.

However, after two days of being back outside, Carlos's little ball-bag started to swell. He had caught an infection and he needed to be kept inside. That first night that we let him in, he just sat in the corner, looking at us, not believing that he was allowed to be there. Every time we stood up, he went to the door expecting to be let out. Eventually after a few hours of nervously sitting upright, we began to see him tire and his eyes began to droop. He was unable to allow himself to relax so he just slept for that first evening standing up. Every so often he would catch his head dropping, and then he would wake himself up again.

After that incident, once Carlos was recovered, we had

to allow all the dogs to sleep inside, so sometimes we end up with all five dogs sleeping on two sofas. When Blue decides it is her time to get up on the sofa, all the other dogs have a look of fear in their eyes, and run for cover. A few months later we came across the discarded bag of testicles, thankfully sealed. It had completely slipped my mind.

The rain continued until March, and when it finally stopped we had had about three months of practically non-stop precipitation, enough to last us a lifetime, and exactly the kind of weather we had moved here to escape from.

Although it was probably the worst winter either Lorna or I had ever experienced, in a funny way we learnt a lot about ourselves, and really started to appreciate our way of life here. Okay, so the roof was leaking and we had to mop, so what? If we had to go to bed at 10 o'clock, and read for an hour before the power ran out, we dealt with it. People have often said to us that they don't think they could live the way we do but I can't imagine it any other way now. We are both healthy, and take pleasure from simple things like walking the dogs on a fresh spring morning, watching the alpacas pronking (when an alpaca gets excited and runs around jumping and leaping in the air, it is called 'pronking') in the evening.

In summer, we might go to town and sit in the park until the early hours of the morning having a drink and a bite to eat and enjoying the cool breeze. Our lives in the UK were so driven by work and 'must-haves' that it is easy to forget the important things.

I can't believe we have managed to convince the people to let us sleep in their house with them. We have even managed to claim a big sofa for ourselves. To be honest sometimes I could live without the little limpy one, he never stops. He is always jumping in my face, or running around in circles, then going to annoy the others, and just when I think I've got some peace and quiet he comes back again. The only time he ever really sleeps is at night, when all the lights go out, then, at least he is quiet.

I'm a bit fed up with this bloody rain though, we don't even get to go out for our walks, all we do is shelter in the dry all day. Sometimes, just for something to do, I run up and down, barking at the cats and the birds in the sky, I don't want to catch them, I'm just shouting at them because it's fun.

Arthur

Chapter 32
Spit Attack

Animal count: Five dogs, two feral cats, two chickens, six alpacas (Cassandra, Lily, Bermuda, Rafa, Galaxy and Eduardo). Sadly we lost Mary-Belle on the only day during that winter when there was no rain. We woke up one day to find it bitterly cold, with a grey sky hanging on the horizon. After an hour or so, to our surprise, snow began to fall, so we went out to photograph the palm tree and olive trees covered in snow, and sadly found that Mary-Belle had died in the night. We had to bury her in her pen. It was a very sad day.

One of the most amazing qualities about alpacas is their amazing mothering instinct. A mother will protect her baby from predators or threats from within the herd or outside. There have been documented reports of alpaca mothers actually killing foxes that have strayed into fields with cria. An alpaca will also give off a shrill alarm call to warn the rest of the herd if they see something that could be a threat to the group. It sounds like a very loud whistle or even a type of scream.

Little Eduardo was starting to grow up now. Thankfully, the rain had finished and finally he was able to get out into the sun, and therefore increase his Vitamin D intake to help his development.

One day we were feeding the alpacas. Eduardo was just starting to want to nibble on the alpaca food, so we had taken to leaving a small amount in the bucket in which we carried the food around to the girls. We had had no problems, but on one occasion he lifted his head up sharply, and propelled the bucket about 15 feet away and it landed with a thump, scaring the girls.

At the time we laughed, but the following day he tried

the same manoeuvre, but this time the handle of the bucket caught on the back of his head and slipped over his neck. Bermuda panicked immediately, letting out an extreme alarm call, seemingly aimed directly at Lorna and I. She obviously thought the bucket was something trying to harm her baby and became visibly distressed. We needed to get the bucket from Eduardo's head as soon as possible!

"Stay there, don't let them past, and I'll grab him and whip the bucket off," I said to Lorna. We always fed them in a corner of the paddock so it was, in theory, easy to pen them in.

As I approached Eduardo, Bermuda gave the loudest, shrillest cry I have ever heard, and she was aiming it right at me. She then directed a large spit directly towards me. I managed to turn around quickly and take it full on my back.

"Phew, that was a close one," I laughed to Lorna.

It is a common misconception that alpacas spit: they rarely spit at humans, unless agitated, but they will spit at each other if tussling or fighting over food. The 'spit' is actually the contents of their stomach. Alpacas are ruminants, and they chew their food over and over, much like goats and sheep, and because this is what comes out when they spit, it smells terrible.

I took a step back and had a rethink.

"What do you think?" I asked Lorna.

"Well, we need to get it off, Bermuda is getting really upset."

"Okay, I guess I'll try again."

This time, I made a grab for Eduardo, knowing that if I could just get hold of him I could get the bucket off him in a matter of seconds.

"Watch out!" Lorna called, but it was too late.

Bermuda made her attack, charging right at me from outside my line of vision, spitting for all she was worth, the green bile coming out of her mouth in rapid, machine gun like shots. It hit me directly in the chest followed swiftly by a shot in the face, right across my nose and mouth. I tried to run, but Bermuda was in the zone and she took up the chase.

"Do something!" I shouted to Lorna in frustration. There I was running around the paddock being chased by Bermuda, and she was just standing there watching, feeling helpless, although (I'm sure) stifling a little snigger.

"What do you want me to do?" she asked.

"I don't know. Distract her maybe. Ugh, it's disgusting. Aaargghhh!"

I was trying to get away, but as I ran she followed, continuing the barrage of foul-smelling spit. Eventually I managed to clamber over the gate and get away. Bermuda was standing there, just staring at me, like a bull stares down a matador; her nostrils were flared and she was breathing hard. I was covered from head to toe in the most putrid gunk imaginable. She really must have dredged up every last bit of it from the pit of all of her stomachs. It was enough to make me retch.

"Okay, any ideas now?" I asked from the other side of the gate.

"Well, let's just give them five minutes to calm down. It's only a bucket, it won't hurt him," Lorna suggested while I tried to scrape off some of the spit.

After a few minutes, watching from a distance, with Bermuda seeming calmer, Lorna suggested going to get some more food to take her mind off of me grabbing Eduardo. It was a great idea and, as soon as she had her head in the bucket, I was able to grab Eduardo, remove the bucket and make my escape.

"Oh my God, you absolutely stink. I think you'd better go and get in the shower - you look like you have been gunged on Noel Edmonds." Lorna was definitely laughing at me now.

Standing there dripping in that foul-smelling concoction, I had no choice but to agree, and trudged off, chalking up another victory to the animals.

This morning was sooo much fun. Mum was having a right

go at the man who brings us food every day. I don't really know what happened, I was eating my food, and then my food thing went around my neck, but Mum got very angry. I was okay, but she was shouting at the man, and every time he tried to come close to me, she ran at him. Then she started spitting at him, and he was running but she wouldn't let him get away. She was so mad, and he was shouting, but I don't understand human.

When she calmed down, the lady gave us some food, and the man grabbed me and took off my food thing from around my neck. He didn't hurt me and Mum didn't shout at him anymore. When the people had gone, I had a little run around with my cousin, and then went to sleep. I've had a lovely day!

Eduardo

Chapter 33
Foal Play

As much as we like our neighbour Ramon, we do not always agree with his animal management techniques. He has a number of horses and they are forever escaping from his land, as his fencing is inadequate. They push the gate open and roam around the countryside, looking for nice, fresh grazing.

One of the ways Spanish farmers try and combat this, and I am sure it happens elsewhere, is to do something called 'hobbling'. They use a piece of rope connected to two ankle cuffs which is supposed to stop the horse from being able to run and jump, meaning they can only take tiny steps, or jump with both front feet at the same time. This is not something we like to see, but sadly we have become accustomed to seeing it here.

Often the horses have over-developed flanks from the extra work they have to do to move around. We often see Ramon's horses congregate outside our fence; they seem to like to come and visit the alpacas and often can be seen nose to nose with one of the boys.

One day in the spring, there were some workmen at the bottom of the track. I was watching them from the window, to see what they were doing.

"Lorna," I called, "It's a bit weird, but I think one of the workmen has got a baby horse with him! Come and see."

Lorna came over to the window. "Hmm, I think you're right. I'm going to ask if I can take a photo." Lorna loves baby animals.

"No, let's get the dogs walked first, then I'll come down with you."

So we walked the dogs and, on our return, grabbed the camera and went out to ask the workmen if we could take

146

a photo of the foal.

As we reached them, we could see the workmen trying to push the foal away from them, as she was getting in their way. We tried to ask if she was theirs, but they didn't seem to want anything to do with her.

"I wonder where she's from then?" Lorna said to me.

"I don't know, maybe I should go and look for the horses, see if they've escaped. Wait here with her, and make sure she is okay."

I went off to look, but after 15 minutes of wandering around the campo there was no sign.

"Maybe we should take her up to the house and I can phone Manuel, and see if he knows what to do," I said.

So I went up to the house, leaving Lorna with a bottle of water, trying to coax the little foal up to the house.

Five minutes later, I was walking back down the hill, only to see Lorna sitting on the ground with the foal's head on her lap. My first thought was, "Oh shit, she's died."

"Is she okay?" I asked.

"She's exhausted," Lorna said. "She's just gone to sleep. What did Manuel say?"

"He is going to phone Ramon, and ask him," I replied.

"I'm worried about her, she seems very weak."

After a few minutes, we woke the foal up, gave her some more water and helped her to her feet. She seemed to get a second wind and we made good progress up the hill and managed to get her into the stable. The phone rang. It was Manuel. It was a short call.

"Manuel says that Ramon has a mare due to birth any day, so he is going to come and see her, then he will bring the mare here. He said maybe we can keep them in the stable for the night. I said that would be fine," I told Lorna.

When Ramon arrived, he was really pleased to see the foal, firstly still alive, and secondly a filly. He tried to explain to us that the mother was a first-time mum, so probably panicked, didn't know what to do and just left the foal behind. Of course, it wouldn't have happened had they been fenced-in securely. He went off to go and collect the mare and returned maybe an hour later, sweating profusely from the trek across the olive groves.

He managed to get her into the stable, with a little cajoling, and she was reunited with the foal. We gave her some oats and a bucket of water, and left them for a few hours, while Ramon promised to check back on them later. We checked on them ourselves about once an hour, and were delighted to see the foal feeding from Mum; we hoped we had saved her life. Ramon popped back and was also pleased to see the foal feeding. He gave the mare some more food and water and said he would be up at some point in the morning to take them back to his farm. We went to bed that night with a warm, positive feeling, really thinking we had done something good.

The next morning, I was up first and went out to check on the foal. I was expecting to see a healthy mother and daughter but sadly, it wasn't to be. When I got there, the foal had died. I had to go back in and tell Lorna. She was truly devastated, but we had truly done all we could. We think that probably the foal just didn't get the first milk in time and, by the time she did finally feed, it was too late for her. It was a real blow. I telephoned Manuel and told him Ramon would need to come and collect the body as soon as possible because we couldn't really do anything while she was still there.

We still see the mare around when the horses escape, and no doubt she will be pregnant again and having another foal in the springtime next year. We will keep our fingers crossed that this time, she will know what to do (and of course that she will do it at home).

Chapter 34
Can't Get Enough of Your Love

By now Rafa was getting bigger and was starting to show signs of adolescence. However, we didn't want to rush into separating him from Cassandra and the other girls too quickly, as we had no 'playmates' for him to live with. One day, we looked out of the window to see Rafa, sitting astride his mother, orgling away ('orgling' is the sound an alpaca makes during mating).

"Erm, I think we had better get outside, Rafa is humping his Mum," I said.

"Oh bugger. I guess that means it's time to separate them?"

We ran outside to interrupt the act, and immediately split Rafa from the group by putting him in a small field, next to the girls, but with a fence and a gate between them to stop him interacting with them. But he could still see them.

"Oh, look at him," Lorna said sadly. Rafa was standing right up against the fence, looking longingly towards his Mum.

"He'll be fine, don't worry. We will just have to get him some friends as soon as possible."

We toyed with the idea of trying to find a miniature donkey for Rafa to have as a companion, but in the end we decided alpacas were best. We contacted a breeder from Gaucin, a small village behind Marbella, and arranged to buy two very cheap, young blue-eyed males, just to keep as company for Rafa. We had to endure two weeks of poor Rafa pining for his Mum, and hardly moving away from the fence, looking forlorn.

After the two weeks of paperwork and arranging transport, Marcus and Alejandro arrived. We moved Rafa and his new buddies around to a new area at the front of the house that we had prepared for them, and all seemed calm. After a few settling in days, despite Rafa being definitely bottom of the pile in terms of hierarchy, they calmed down into a good routine, slowly munching their way through the weeds and rough grass in their paddock.

One day, we had been into Montoro to do our weekly shop, and on our way up the hill to the house, I was unable to see the boys in their paddock.

"That's strange," I said. "I can't see the boys."

As we passed the girls' paddock we could see why.

"There they are, bloody hell, they've escaped." Lorna said.

The boys had indeed escaped and we were looking at our three girls, sitting calmly along the floor in a line, all facing away from us while Rafa, Marcus and Alejandro were having a 'Barry White' moment. We jumped out of the car hoping that it had only just started and shouted, yelled and clapped loudly, trying to stop the boys. Although it was very difficult, I might add, we did somehow manage to chase them back to their paddock.

We had read in our research that usually, alpaca boys don't become fertile until around three years old. Given that all these boys were young, we hoped that the mating would prove unsuccessful. After all the disasters we had suffered we just were not ready for more emotional turmoil. As the weeks passed, the girls' behaviour didn't seem to change and we put it out of our minds, believing that we had had a lucky escape.

Looking back now, we could (and probably should) have done some spit-offs with the girls. This is a way of testing if a female alpaca is pregnant; by introducing her to a male. If she is not pregnant, she will invariably sit down for him to mate her. If she is pregnant, she will spit at him. I'm sure there are many men who will sympathise with the poor male alpaca that gets that job.

Chapter 35
Alpaca Chasing

Animal count: Five dogs, two feral cats, two chickens and eight alpacas (Cassandra, Lily, Bermuda, Rafa, Galaxy, Eduardo, Marcus and Alejandro).

In March, Lorna made the trip back, this time to be there (well, not actually there this time) for the birth of her next grandchild. Mark's baby was due any day and we were expecting the worst to happen when Lorna was away, so I decided to not to try to do too much, just stay at home and make sure all the animals were all right. However, one day, Miguel pulled up outside, just for a little chat about the weather and the olives, and I had opened the gate. When I came back in, obviously I had forgotten to lock the gate behind me. We very rarely have visitors, so security is often the last thing on our minds.

After an hour or so, the dogs were being very quiet and everything seemed calm, so I went out to check that all was as it should be. To my surprise, the alpaca boys were not where they should be, again. I couldn't see them anywhere and the front gate had been pushed slightly ajar. A slight wave of panic hit me, as I realised that the boys (that's the non-fence challenging alpaca boys), had gone under their paddock fence, found their way around to the front gate and pushed it open. God knows where they were, or how long they had been gone.

As luck would have it, Miguel was still around, working as always on his tractor, and he pointed me in the direction of his house, where there is a large area of land with a reasonable covering of grass. Our animals are used to living on dry food, hay and alfalfa and whatever grass we manage to grow on our land, so if there is any possibility to feed on a patch of lush vegetation, that is obviously too good an opportunity to miss.

So I trudged over to the boys, trying to work out how on earth I was going to herd them back to our house. The normal food trick was going to be no good: they were out to get the food that was there, which was a better option than I could offer. Without fencing, grabbing an alpaca is nigh on impossible as they are flight animals. That is to say, if they are frightened, they run. They don't fight, they get away, and when they run, boy can they run!

After a few minutes' walk, they came into sight, and I breathed a sigh of relief; at least I knew where they were. However the lack of fencing around made it difficult and I didn't want to upset them and chase them further away. I enlisted the tractor-driving Miguel to follow them and slowly usher them back in the direction of the house. Although he was keen, while I was trying to be quiet and not upset them, he was using his Spanish farmer's animal call which sounds a little bit like a Red Indian attack cry. Of course every time he did this the alpacas freaked a little and we were back to square one.

After a few attempts I managed to get him to be quiet, and luckily good old Ramon drove past so we managed to get him involved too. We had to endure the initial attempts of Ramon believing himself to be master of the animals and trying to grab the alpacas, but they were far too quick for him. So, on the bonnet of his dirty old pickup truck, I sketched out a plan with my finger. I drew the gates to our house and the alpacas. Then I drew three little stick men, one to represent me, behind the alpacas driving them forward, and two more either side of the alpacas to keep them from going left or right.

I gestured to Ramon and Miguel that under no circumstances were they to shout or call. They were to keep their arms up, and wave them around if the alpacas tried to pass them. After about 15 minutes of maybe ten metres forward, five metres back, and various eating stops for the boys, we crept over the hill nearing the gate. I was praying that no cars went past, because no matter what we are doing, our local farmers always toot their horns and if that happened I knew we would lose them again.

I had left the gate open, both to the fence surrounding the house and the gate to the alpacas' paddock. As it came into view, and I was trying to figure out the next move, the three boys just trotted back into their paddock without any fuss or encouragement from us. Alpacas do have a way of making you look stupid sometimes, as if they know what they are doing. Sometimes we might be trying to clip toenails, or the vet might be taking a blood sample, and the animal will fight for maybe 30 minutes and just when you think it's an impossible task, you say to yourself, one more go. Then they just stand there and let you do it as though nothing has happened. It is the most frustrating feeling in the world.

I once saw a documentary about the making of a film that featured some alpacas amongst other animals, and the animal trainer said that alpacas were the hardest animals he had ever worked with, much harder than even lions and tigers. They just do whatever they want to do.

Chapter 36
Flystrike

Animal count: Five dogs, two feral cats, three new feral kittens (we decided to name them Andres, Fernando and Sergio, in honour of the Spanish World Cup winning team), two chickens and eight alpacas.

The worst thing about living in Andalucía, for me, and much worse than the searing heat, are the flies. During the summer and into October, flies become the most annoying thing in my life. No matter how many doors and windows that you close behind you, some always get in, and by the end of summer they even seem to become immune to sprays.

One of the things you hear about when researching farm animals, and talking to other owners, is something called flystrike. Flystrike is when an animal has a wound, or a collection of hair matted with faeces, and a blowfly comes and lays its eggs in the wound, whereupon they hatch and become maggots. If this isn't caught, the cycle can keep going: when the maggots become flies, they lay more eggs and the problem escalates.

One morning, we went out to feed the alpacas and Lorna noticed some blood on the back of Cassandra's legs.

"Err, Alan, have a look at Cassandra, there seems to be some blood around her lady-bits!"

"Oh God, what now? Yep, I can see it, let's get a hold of her."

We closed them in their field shelter, where we always feed them, and, while Lorna got a hold of Cassandra, I lifted her tail for a better look.

"She seems to have cut herself, I need to take a better look. Hang on, try and keep her still."

As I looked closer, and used my hands to look into the

wound, I could see what looked like bubbles. I didn't really know what they were, but I had an idea.

"I think she's got flystrike and there are eggs in there. Maybe we should get some tweezers and get them out. I don't mind doing it."

So we got the tweezers, but I couldn't get hold of the eggs, and once again we were forced to phone Manuel, and make the hour-long round trip to collect him. On the journey I explained the problem to him. He was convinced it was flystrike but would check when he arrived.

Lorna again held Cassandra, while I watched as Manuel dealt with her. When he looked, he could see what I saw.

I said, "I think there are eggs here," and pointed to the bubbles.

"No, they are the maggots. It is the back end; they breathe through there and eat the dead flesh from the front, burrowing their way in."

So what I thought had been eggs were in actual fact the back ends of the maggots, about two days into their life cycle. It sounded horrific, and we were really worried about Cassandra, but as Manuel took hold of the maggots with long tweezers, and pulled them out one by one, they left behind little holes where they had been, like a little honeycomb. It was very interesting in a morbid way, and left a very clean wound which was easy to manage. We gave Cassandra an antibiotic injection, and had a daily cleaning and cream ritual, but in no time the wound was healing.

Sadly, about a week after the antibiotics, Cassandra aborted a very small cria early one morning. Obviously, she had become pregnant during the boys' escape. Although we were a little upset, we knew that the pregnancy had not been planned, and it was better that she was healthy. Of course, as she had been pregnant, this did raise the issue that the other two girls were also pregnant, and if so, they should be due around Christmas. We talked about Lily's previous premature birth, and we decided that if it was meant to be, all would be okay. We just had to

155

cross our fingers.

A week or so later, we actually had a repeat of the flystrike problem, this time, in a wound in between the toes on Rafa's foot. We were able to deal with it ourselves this time, and his foot made a quick and full recovery. So far, they have been our only instances of this horrendous problem, but it is something we are always on the lookout for in the summer: it can manifest itself so quickly.

Chapter 37
Eggs in the Morning?

Although we had had more than our fair share of setbacks and heartache, and we had put the house on the market just to see if anything happened (the worldwide recession was starting to bite), we were beginning to settle into our new life. We had no money, really no money apart from for essentials, shopping and gas plus petrol for the car.

We could no longer afford to go out for meals, or to buy each other presents for birthdays and Christmas, although we always put some aside for presents for loved ones. But yet, as we walked the dogs in the mornings, breathing the fresh morning air in springtime or enjoying a thunderstorm of rain at the end of summer, our lives had really changed. We no longer slaved away at our jobs, never seeing each other, and having no time to appreciate life.

Instead of having the latest innovative mobile phone or device, we still have the original phone we bought when we arrived, now well into its fifth year of life, held together by a raggedy piece of gaffer tape.

If we could just sort out our finances, we could stay here forever. We have certainly grown accustomed to the way of life here, and when we talk to people who say, "We would love to do this one day, maybe when the kids are older," we always groan to ourselves or allow each other a little smirk knowing it will never happen. Why wait until the kids are older? If you move when they are young, they will learn the language in no time, probably within six months. Why make a three, five or even ten-year plan? Who ever knows what is around the corner.

As our two little chickens had managed to avoid the threat of any local wildlife having them for dinner, we decided to add to our brood by going out one day to a farm in Cordoba where we had heard it was possible to buy all sorts of chickens. We were enjoying the few eggs we got from our two, so we decided half a dozen more would be an added attraction around the farm (plus we have kind of fallen in love with chickens, they are just so funny).

We headed out one day in early summer in Frank, the mobile greenhouse, and made for the farm we'd been told about. When we pulled off the road, I think we had been expecting a large warehouse, comprising neat rows of cages, with all different types of chickens. But when we pulled into the yard, things could have not been more different. There were crates spread about the floor with rocks on top to stop individual cockerels from escaping. We could see large wheeled cages, similar to supermarket delivery cages, with hundreds of young, balding chickens, geese and ducks.

We felt sorry for these confined birds, but we had come here to get chickens, so we had to ask the man. He brought us over what could only be described as a chicken menu, on which he pointed out the best breeds to live in the campo, for producing eggs, not meat.

We chose three pairs of different coloured birds: two black/brown, two white, and two speckled grey girls. They were brought out unceremoniously hanging by their feet from the man's hands, swinging as though they had had their necks wrung and were to be plucked for dinner. But he thrust them into a cardboard box and they huddled in a corner, starting to cluck a little. We loaded them in the car, and set off.

As I am sure many holidaymakers and expats will tell you, road signs in Spain can be haphazard to say the least, so in my haste to get home, I took the first turning signposted back to Cordoba. As we followed the road, however, winding through fields of hay and sunflowers, we realised we had gone wrong. We could see the motorway, about 300 metres away, running parallel with the small road we were now following. It was over 40 degrees, and I was beginning to panic that by the time we got home, the chickens would be ready-roasted.

Eventually, after about 40 extra kilometres of countryside driving, we managed to get back on to the motorway and I put my foot down to get us home quickly.

When we got there and opened the box, it was a relief to find them all still with us. We carried the box to the field where the 'chicken shed' is, and let them out. It was strange, but they seemed to move as one. They all huddled into a corner, clucking and pecking at each other, and although we tried to move them around, going behind them and clapping and shouting, they moved together, as though they were stuck together. We worked out that they must have been living in such cramped conditions that it was a real culture shock for them to be free, and although we would have loved to save more animals from a horrid life, we are pleased that they now have a great time, running around with the alpacas. We get plenty of eggs as a reward!

Chapter 38
Poor Lily

Animal count: Five dogs, five feral cats, eight chickens (we decided to name the new chickens after some of our elderly relatives, so the six new ones were named Audrey, Eileen, Mabel, Jess, Marge and Jean, and they joined Beyonce and J-lo) and eight alpacas.

All of a sudden, at the beginning on November, almost a year to the day since Lily lost her last baby, we were outside letting the girls do some 'gardening' for us, by eating the weeds that had grown up with the autumn rain. I had said to Lorna recently that I was sure Lily was looking a bit rounder, but we were not convinced, because, of course, her fleece was building up with the cold weather.

"I think you'd better see this," I said to Lorna, watching Lily roll around in the dust. "Look, her boobies are huge. I think that confirms it, she's pregnant."

"Oh God, let's hope she can hold on for a bit then, she isn't due till Christmas."

So I rushed in to have a look online to see how early alpacas come into milk before they are due to birth. My mind was put at rest when I read that it can be at least a month before the birth, and Lily was about six weeks away from being due.

"I do hope she can hold on this time, it was so awful last time. I just want it to be okay for her," Lorna said.

The following week, we popped out to run some errands in town. We hadn't left until late morning, and all seemed fine. On our return, I was reversing into our courtyard to unload some shopping, and I could see Lily sitting in the girls' stable with what looked like a nervous little dog next to her. I was out of the car quickly.

"I think there's a dog in the stable," I shouted "Oh

shit, nope, it's a baby. Lily has had her baby."

Inside the stable, sitting next to Lily, was a little brown female cria. We turned her over to give her a clean, but noticed that she was bleeding from her umbilical cord and there were patches of blood on the floor of the stable. We couldn't be sure if it was from the baby or from the birth.

Knowing we needed to stop the bleeding, I tried to phone Manuel but there was no answer. So I decided to dash back to the town, and look for him. In any case I would have had to go and collect him to bring him back.

When I got to the surgery, there was no sign of Manuel, and I again tried to phone. Still no answer. I tried another vet in town but he was not there either. I was now in panic mode and decided that it was more important to get back home so we could try to stop the bleeding, and hopefully get the baby up and feeding in those crucial first hours.

When I returned, Lorna was a bit distressed to see that Manuel was not with me, but I explained that I had looked for both vets, there was no sign, so I had made the decision to get back and try to stop the bleeding.

After looking online again, there were instances cited of people pegging the wound closed. So I found a plastic bag clip, sterilised it in hot water and iodine, and used that to seal the wound. Thankfully it did manage to stop the bleeding although we were unclear how much blood she had lost.

Our next job was to get some colostrum into her if she was going to have any chance of surviving. We got hold of Lily, checked her for milk and there was some there. Slowly we managed to milk her into a plastic jug and then used a syringe to feed it to the baby, millilitre by millilitre. Every half hour or so we did this until it started to get dark, then we tended to them every hour during the night.

At one stage in the night, Lily's mothering instincts seemed to kick in and she was nudging at the baby, trying to help it find the 'milk bar', as it tends to get called. We looked at each other and smiled, hoping that mother nature would kick in for us, and things would be okay. It was 5 am and I was exhausted, knowing that I was probably going to have to drive and get Manuel later that morning so decided to have a couple of hours sleep.

Lorna couldn't bring herself to sleep; she didn't want me to go out and find the baby dead and have to come back and tell her, so she stayed up and checked on them. At about 7 am, Lorna came down and woke me up.

"I don't think she is going to last much longer," she said. "She's gone very weak, and her breathing has changed. I think we just need to try and make her as comfortable as possible until she goes."

I got dressed and went outside to be with Lorna, not wanting her to go through it on her own. When I saw how the baby was breathing and unable to lift her head, I realised Lorna was right, and we sat with her and Lily, waiting for the end. Lily just sat next to us, looking forlorn. I think she probably knew; she was just waiting too.

Hours passed, and every so often the little one's eyes would close and the breathing would stop, only for it to kick in again a few seconds later. She certainly was a fighter. After a few hours, I managed to speak to Manuel and Lorna and I decided that it would be best if I went to collect him, and at least we could put the baby to sleep: it was going on too long now, and it wasn't fair.

As I was driving home with Manuel and was explaining that all we really wanted was for him to give her an injection to put her to sleep, Lorna phoned to say that she had died. I could hear the tears in Lorna's voice, but was glad the decision was taken out of our hands.

On our return, Lorna explained that she had been sitting on the floor with Lily and the baby, and the baby had taken one last breath, and a cough, and that was it, she was gone. Lily seemed to know immediately and let out a distraught cry - that was enough to make Lorna cry.

Manuel had a look at the baby and tried to explain to us that because she was so premature she had very little chance, she would not have been fully developed. We decided to give Lily some antibiotics, more as a precaution than anything else. As Lorna was holding her, I said, "Look, she's crying." Lily had a single tear rolling down each cheek. I have never seen or heard of that before in an animal, and it was particularly heart-wrenching, as it was the second time it had happened to Lily.

I took the body of the baby away and buried it out on our land, away from the house. This time, Lily knew what had happened; we didn't have the horrible humming and crying every time we went into the paddock. Although she was quiet for a few days, she seemed to recover well. After further research we decided that it might have helped, although there is no guarantee, if we had been able to give her some blood plasma from the blood of another alpaca. One of the other farms in Andalucía had a small supply so we decided to get a batch, just in case, knowing that soon Bermuda could soon be giving birth.

One day, we hope very much that Lily will be able to go full-term and have a healthy cria with us. She so deserves it.

Chapter 39
Santa's Christmas Delivery

It was the run-up to Christmas and our nerves, by now, were shot to pieces. We spent our days doing almost hourly checks on Bermuda, our paranoia taking over as we awaited the next birth. We had decided that if we were at all worried about Bermuda's new baby, we would ask Manuel to give her the plasma we had acquired, a belts and braces approach that we felt necessary after everything that had happened.

It was the second Christmas since Kaci had been born and Lorna was excited, as Frankie and Chris had been able to get time off work to come over and spend Christmas with us here. That meant Christmas Day with Kaci, so Lorna had something to be excited about.

Yet again, in December, the rain started, but thankfully it lasted only a couple of weeks, finishing on Christmas Day and staying bright and dry for the rest of Frankie's visit, However, given our luck, I'm sure you're aware that not everything would go smoothly…

On Christmas Eve we awoke to foul weather, rain coming down and the paddocks thoroughly soaked, and we were covered in mud from just feeding the alpacas. Our morning check of Bermuda had shown up nothing to be concerned about, so we lit a log fire, and were sitting around, enjoying some quiet family time.

At about 5 pm, I went out on the terrace to check Bermuda, and could immediately see that things had changed. She was at the poo pile, straining, and I thought to myself, 'Right this is it.'

Lorna and I put on our pack-a-macs and went out in the rain. From start to finish Bermuda gave birth, unassisted, in around ten minutes and the birth was, as they say, textbook. We scooped up the little boy, sprayed his navel, and moved him in to the stable. How very apt, on Christmas Eve!

Bermuda of course followed, and we put Cassandra and Lily in too. We gave them all fresh bedding and a good supply of food and water and settled in to watch. It was starting to get dark now.

Although it can take a few hours for the baby to get strong enough to find the right place to feed, our nerves had gone and, after only about two hours, we felt Bermuda wasn't very interested. So we phoned Manuel to ask if he would come and give the new baby the plasma we had. After a couple of attempts to get him, he called back to say he was at a party and couldn't help us, we would have to go to Cordoba University to see the emergency vet there. We decided to phone Peter, to ask if he could call ahead for us, as he speaks better Spanish than both of us, and warn them we were coming. We loaded the baby into the car and started on the journey.

Peter phoned about ten minutes later.

"Alan, they said there is no one there who can do it. They said under no circumstances go to the university."

"You're joking? What do we do now?"

"They gave me the number of an emergency horse vet who is on call tonight. I have spoken to him, explained the situation, and he is going to meet you in the car park of the Cordoba football stadium in 30 minutes."

"Okay, thanks Peter, that's great. Does he speak English?"

"No, well only a little. Good luck, we are crossing everything for you." I hung up the phone.

"Would you believe it? We have to go and meet a horse vet, in the car park of the football stadium, and I guess we will follow him to his surgery from there," I explained to Lorna.

"Doesn't get any easier living here, does it?"

"Nope," I replied.

So off we went, eventually getting to the car park, and driving around looking for another car. After a few minutes a car pulled up, but by now it was totally dark, and raining and there was no one around. As the vet stepped out of the car and shook hands with us, we tried to explain, with broken Spanish, pointing and gesturing that we wanted to get the plasma into the baby, by IV drip. That was all we wanted. He seemed to understand. Then, he started to pull on a green surgical vest top and, to our astonishment, proceeded to put on a type of headband with a spotlight attached, and manoeuvre the baby into the best light in the back of the car. We suddenly realised that this emergency horse vet didn't have a surgery; he was used to dealing with things in the countryside. We looked at each other. We could both tell neither of us was happy with the situation, but we were so scared of losing the baby we went with it.

The vet or course, had never seen an alpaca before, so finding a vein in the leg in which to put the IV was difficult to say the least. Having seen Manuel struggle when ours had been ill, I knew this was crucial, so we were patient and eventually the vet managed to strike lucky and got into the vein. He attached the bag of plasma, but it wouldn't flow. The last needle set he had wasn't working, so he taped the catheter to the baby's leg, hoping it would stay there, and asked us to follow him to where he kept his stock.

We followed for five minutes, and eventually pulled into a small underground car park, where there was an ambulance parked up.

While we were driving Lorna said to me, "If he doesn't get it going in a few more minutes, I think we should go back. Put him back with Bermuda, and hope mother nature does her bit."

"Okay," I agreed.

He got a needle set but, when we looked at the catheter, it had come out of the vein. We had to make a decision: we didn't want to cause unnecessary pain and discomfort to the cria. So we asked the emergency vet to stop working and said we would take him home. It was late now, and would be gone 10 pm by the time we got to the Olive Mill.

166

On the journey the cria was strong and moving about so we had high hopes that things might be okay, but of course at the back of our minds were all the other losses that had occurred.

"We'll put him back in with Bermuda, leave them penned in together for the night and hope that her instinct kicks in, and he finds the milk."

"I think that's all we can do," Lorna said sadly.

We shot back as quickly as possible and introduced the cria back to Bermuda. Although she hadn't seemed interested before, it was as if taking the baby away had kicked in her instinct and she recognised him immediately. He went straight up to her and looked for food. After a few minutes, he found the teats and seemed to be suckling. We were happy to leave them to it for the night, and kept our fingers crossed that he had got the colostrum in time - and that he would still be alive in the morning.

We got back in to find Frankie and Chris with dinner on the table, and very welcome it was too.

After a terrible night's sleep, I was awake at first light and out to see how the baby was doing. I was so pleased to see him, up and about, bright as a button and feeding from Bermuda as though nothing had happened the day before.

Of course Lorna was excited to hear the news, and was able to get up and enjoy Christmas morning with her family for the first time in two years, and with Kaci there as well, everything was more exciting.

We had to name the new arrival, and to be honest there was only two contenders: Santa and Jesus (pronounced hey-zoos as the Spanish do). Jesus would have worked with the stable and everything but in the end we decided Santa was more appropriate and easy for people to remember.

That Christmas day was probably one of Lorna's best, and most memorable, and it could only have been bettered if Mark had been able to be here with little Maisie.

With everything we had been through, this felt like a new beginning. Yes, things had been hard, and things had gone wrong, but we had dealt with it and come out the other side stronger and better people. We love our life here, and we love breeding alpacas, even though sometimes it feels like the most heartbreaking job in the world.

Hopefully, one day soon, things will pick up in the world: people will have money to spend and maybe, just maybe, our plan to make a living at breeding these amazing animals will come to fruition. In the meantime, we just have to enjoy our back-to-basics lifestyle, living off-grid and trying to understand this crazy country we now call home. Who knows what the next few years will bring or where we will be in two years time, but you can be sure of one thing, our lives have changed once and for all.

Final animal count: Five dogs (Geri, Carlos, Blue, Arthur and Miliko), five feral cats (Barb, R Denise, Andres, Fernando and Sergio), eight chickens (Beyonce and J-lo, Audrey, Eileen, Mabel, Jess, Marge and Jean) and nine alpacas (Cassandra, Lily, Bermuda, Rafa, Galaxy, Eduardo, Marcus, Alejandro and of course little Santa!)

If you enjoyed *Seriously Mum, What's an Alpaca?*
please consider leaving a review.
Thank you!

Also by Alan Parks, the sequel,
Seriously Mum, Where's that Donkey?

Available in paperback and e-book editions

So, what happened next?

Turn to the page to find out...

An excerpt from the sequel,
Seriously Mum, Where's that Donkey?

Have you ever licked a toad?

On the ground was the biggest toad I have ever seen; he was about the size of a dinner plate. His fat body glistened in the sun and our dog Geri, who had travelled over from Brighton with us was becoming very interested. We decided to leave the toad to it, took Geri and went and had lunch. When we returned, Mr Toad had gone.

Frogs and toads are a fact of life here: our little stream seems to be a breeding ground for them in springtime and, as dusk falls, you can hear the croaks and ribbits of the night-time mating sessions. We have a water deposit outside the part of the Olive Mill in which we live and there is also an overflow drain to prevent the water from becoming stagnant. Even in summer this drain is a damp haven, and every year we have had a toad 'move in' for the long, hot months. Maybe he is even that same toad. We occasionally get a glimpse of His Toadness - he is, as I said, rather big - and over the autumn months when it is time to clean out the deposit, we always find the odd tadpole (maybe Mr Toad is female then!) which we turf out to be washed back downstream.

During the rare occasions when we have terrible weather here in Andalucia, it can be a bit grim and depressing, but thankfully it doesn't happen too often. It was, however, on one such day that we had the toad experience from hell.

The day started like most. I was woken at about 8.15 by a cacophony of dogs' howling to be let out. I got up and opened the door for them and went back to bed. Fifteen minutes later, I woke to find Lorna getting up as Geri could be heard moved moving about. We are pretty sure Geri is deaf as she doesn't join in the barking sessions unless she is awake and can see the others doing it. We have to get to Geri quickly: she is 15 now and once she is up she is liable to poo and wee all over the living room. The alarm was due to go off anytime so we thought we might as well get up. Outside the weather was damp and grey, as it had been for a few days. I flicked a light switch.

"Great," I said. "No electrics!"

Living off-grid, we depend on solar panels for our electricity. We have a bank of batteries to store what we generate, but if it is cloudy for a few days in a row, our stores start to deplete. Sometimes we can go for days with the fridge turned off to save power.

I fumbled around for some clothes that were not wet or damp, and got dressed. First job of the morning is to walk the dogs. We have to do this in two shifts: Blue and Arthur first, as they are so big, and then the little ones. I always walk Blue as she is strong and built like an ox, while Lorna takes Arthur. We have to be on guard in case any horses have been around and have done their business. For some reason, this is of great attraction to the dogs and if Blue and Arthur want to charge off and roll in it, we can't stop them!

Half an hour later we returned for the second stint. Miliko was crazily excited, running round in small circles and jumping up while Carlos was whipping everybody into a frenzy with his barking. Geri was oblivious. "In your own time, Geri!"

We returned at about 10am to find that although still cloudy, the electricity had come back on. Although the fridge had been off for two days, we could at least get online. When the weather is inclement, we can't do any washing as the washing machine uses a lot of power so we have to recycle clothes once we run out of clean things. However, if there's no sunshine, it's not hot, so they don't get sweaty. We try and do outside tasks in between the heavy showers and storms.

By mid-afternoon on this particular day, however, it was so cold and horrible that we decided the best place to be was under the duvet, so we retired for a siesta for a couple of hours with a mug of hot chocolate and a book. At about 6pm, just as it was getting dark, we treated ourselves to the generator for the evening. We can't afford the petrol to run it all day, but at least it meant we could watch a little TV, turn the fridge on and for a few hours have a bit of comfort.

We were in our living room watching TV, turned up loud over the din of the generator and Miliko (now affectionately known as 'Shit Face' because he likes to eat, well you know…) started going mad. Now, this in itself is nothing unusual. If the chickens come too close, he barks at them; if the kittens are in sight, he barks at them; if the young alpacas fight, he barks at them. You get the idea. But after a few minutes of constant barking, he wasn't stopping. So I picked up a torch and went out to investigate. It was a dank, wet night and because of the clouds there was no moonlight. We were in total darkness. I finally located Miliko and could see him barking at the ground in front of him…

Contacts and Links

We welcome contact from anybody interested in hearing more about our life, or about alpacas in general.

Email
lornaalpacaselsol@gmail.com

Facebook
http://www.facebook.com/al.parks

Facebook Page
http://www.facebook.com/whatsanalpaca

Blog
www.whats-an-alpaca.com

Lorna's Blog
www.lornaslifeinspain.blogspot.com

Twitter
https://twitter.com/alpacabook

Pinterest
http://pinterest.com/alanparks/

If you would like to visit us and the alpacas here in Andalucia, we would love to hear from you.

Acknowledgments

This is my first attempt at writing a book, and I hope it's been successful, only time will tell. I would of course like to thank everyone who has helped and supported me through this exciting, nerve-racking and sleep depriving process.

Lorna and I would like to say thank you to my Mum, Linda and my Grandmother Renee for the support they have shown us during our time in Spain. Without their help and support in so many ways, we would not still be here living the dream, and occasional nightmares, that this life throws at us.

Immense thanks to Victoria Twead and www.AntPress.org for help, advice and support whenever we needed it, and to our great friend Jo Roddick for editing the book, taking time away from her family and extremely busy work schedule to help us out.

We will always be grateful to our good friend Trudy Mills who very kindly donated a laptop to us, so Lorna would not get withdrawal symptoms if she could not get onto Facebook and check in with the family regularly. Without that kindness, the book probably wouldn't exist.

Thank you Anja, Shelley, Sue, Christine, Bea, Gaynor, Theresa, Pat, Robyn and Kerri who agreed to read the story to ensure it would be at least a little interesting to people... We hope!

Thank you, and sorry to Lorna's wonderful children, Mark and Frankie Penfold, who have both had to live through some wonderful and some difficult times, and not always had their Mum beside them, when they really needed her. Also, to her beautiful grandgirlies Kaci and Maisie, Nanny wishes she could see you more often, you mean the world to her.

Last, but not least, I, Alan, would like to say thank you

to my Dad, who died eight years ago, but without his fight and dignity during illness I would not have had the bravery to live my life for today, and never wait until it is too late! Without that we wouldn't be here now.

Alan Parks

About the Author

Alan Parks was born in Eastbourne in 1978, and moved to Andalucia with his partner, Lorna, in 2008. Since then they have endured good and bad times in equal measure. In 2012 Alan published his first memoir, *Seriously Mum, What's an Alpaca?* Owing to its popularity, he was encouraged to write this sequel describing even more of his and Lorna's (mis)adventures.

A Recommendation

If, after reading this book, you are interested in the world of alpacas, please take a look at the website of our good friend Tim Hey, of Inca Alpaca in the UK.

Amberley Farm, Higher Drove, Chilfrome,

Dorchester, Dorset, England DT2 0HU

www.incaalpaca.co.uk

Printed in Great Britain
by Amazon.co.uk, Ltd.,
Marston Gate.